Reluctant to Read?

Editor JOHN L. FOSTER

Ward Lock Educational

ISBN 0 7062 3642 4

First published 1977
Reprinted 1978

Set in 11 on 13 point Monotype Imprint
by Latimer Trend & Company Ltd Plymouth
and printed by Biddles Ltd, Guildford, Surrey
for Ward Lock Educational
116 Baker Street, London W1M 2BB
A member of the Pentos Group
Made in Great Britain

Contents

Acknowledgments

The editor and publishers would like to thank the following for their permission to reproduce copyright material: Keith Bardgett for 'The nature of reluctance' © Keith Bardgett 1977; Geoff Fox for 'Reading fiction – starting where the kids are' © Geoff Fox 1977; Robert Leeson for 'A reluctant literature?' © Robert Leeson 1977; Sheila Ray for 'The development of the teenage novel' © Sheila Ray 1977; Olive Robinson for 'From remedial to reader' © Olive Robinson 1977; *The Sunday Times Magazine* for the use of the article 'Paperbacks: Success Stories' by Suzanne Hodgart.

Preface

Over the past ten years growing concern about the standard of reading achieved by secondary school pupils has focused attention not only on children whose reading ability is poor, but also on those who have the ability to read books, but choose not to do so. There has been a widespread debate on what has become known as the problem of the reluctant reader and a number of writers and publishers have produced books and series specially designed to appeal to less motivated readers. Teachers and librarians have sought to identify books that have a wide appeal and by making them readily available have sought to foster the development of the reading habit among pupils who can read, but who demonstrate a reluctance to turn to books either for pleasure or for information. The articles in this book consider the philosophy that lies behind a policy of tackling the problem of reluctance by making a special provision for such readers, re-examine the nature and causes of reluctance to read and give details of titles and of approaches that have proved successful in the classroom.

In the opening article Keith Bardgett challenges some of the assumptions that are often made about the nature of reluctance and argues that the root cause lies in our attitudes as teachers rather than in the attitudes of the pupils. His argument that it is necessary to start where the pupils want to begin is echoed in the second article, in which Geoff Fox looks at the process of reading and argues that because the reader's response is both unique and unpredictable any policy aimed at overcoming reluctance must involve 'starting where the kids are'. Robert Leeson's article 'A reluctant literature?' complements those by

Keith Bardgett and Geoff Fox. Writing from an author's standpoint Robert Leeson suggests that if many young people do not become book-readers then it is because writers are failing to communicate to their audience and that 'the inadequacy is ours, not theirs'.

In 'The development of the teenage novel' Sheila Ray explains why the teenage novel emerged in Britain in the 1960s and gives a factual account, detailing titles and trends, of how it has developed since. In my own article I outline a secondary school's policy towards reluctant readers aged eleven to sixteen and give a fully annotated list of popular titles, which also includes detailed suggestions for further reading. Finally, Olive Robinson, the head of a remedial department in a comprehensive school, describes an approach to the problem of the underachieving reader in the secondary school and lists some of the series that have proved useful in helping such pupils not only to develop their reading skills but to learn to enjoy reading.

John L. Foster

1977

1 The nature of reluctance

Keith Bardgett
*Head of the English Department, Denbigh School,
Milton Keynes*

One of the significant advances in the teaching of reading in our comprehensive schools over the past fifteen years has been the attention given to the reluctant reader and his problems. Identifying the reluctant readers and trying to get them interested in books was an important step forward. But there is a danger that we might be overhasty in categorising children as reluctant readers. What exactly do we mean when we use the term reluctant reader? Might it not be possible that the use of the term blurs our vision, and prevents us from seeing some of the important factors which are responsible for children's reluctance?

My main argument is that the term reluctant reader is too vague to be of much use to us, because it begs a lot of arguably more serious problems. It is my contention that these problems are not so much in the pupils, as in educational theory and practice. Certain it is that if a solution is to be found, it is teachers, and not pupils, who must find it.

There are many reasons for reluctance, such as peer-group pressure, missed schooling at earlier crucial years, and parental dismissal of fiction as 'soppy', but here I want to concentrate on five areas which, when taken together, illustrate the complexity of the problem.

1 The aesthetic approach to reading
This is a hangover from our own formal education. We are rightly concerned with quality, but in what is that quality to be found? The academic answer is, of course, in the 'literature'

studied. 'Good' literature is that which we ourselves have studied. It is part of our heritage. It has survived the ravages of time. It is written by 'accepted' authors, usually of long standing. It is literature of which T. S. Eliot writes:

> A mature literature, therefore, has a history behind it; a history is not merely a chronicle, an accumulation of manuscripts and writings of this kind and that, but an ordered, though unconscious, progress of a language to realise its own potentialities, within its own limitations.[1]

and, elsewhere:

> The existing monuments form an ideal order among themselves, which is modified by the introduction of the new (the really new) work of art among them.[2]

This 'vision' is clearly metaphysical. The order in which Eliot sees works of art is not the order in which a library is set out, and I doubt if any two people could agree on an order when it came down to specific texts. Again, to how many of our pupils would the phrase 'an ordered, though unconscious, progress of a language to realize its own potentialities, within its own limitations' mean very much? I don't want to be misunderstood here. I am not doubting that some works of literature are 'better' (in this accepted sense) than others. I am far from certain, however, that these should be our main concern as English teachers. Should we not, rather, be concerned with the quality of response; the quality of the written and oral work done by our pupils? It is far from self-evident that 'good' stimulus material will produce 'good' work, especially when we think of the reluctant reader. Given the choice between, for example, Hamlet's 'To be or not to be' and an extract from Alvarez' book on suicide, *The Savage God* (Weidenfeld and Nicholson, 1971), I know which would produce the most lively and genuine response from a large number of pupils. The question being posed here is this: do we not

2

base our judgement of who is reluctant on their ability or reluctance to read what we call English Literature?

2 The inverse Oliver syndrome

Being well read, we all know that, when hungry, Oliver Twist had the audacity to ask for more. A nutrition expert would probably say that more of the disgusting gruel would have done him more harm than good, but that is by the way. Do we not sometimes do the opposite? This course is sticking in their throats, so let us water it down. Give them the same only less. I think this is at least part of the explanation for the explosion of text books consisting of extracts from the masters, either in straight anthologies, or suitably edited, annotated, and swelled to the requisite length with comprehension questions such as, 'What does "peripheral" mean on line forty-nine? Put it in a sentence to show that you know what it means.' There is no need to labour the point. If Shakespeare doesn't always 'work' (and why on earth should he? He wasn't writing just to give us stimulus material), I see no reason why one scene or speech taken out of context should be any more successful. Even worse, in my view, is the existence of watered-down or edited classics, and rewrites putting the 'story' into easy language.

3 Selective vision

This operates both consciously and unconsciously. At its most basic, one can say that 'reading' has taken place if someone has looked at a printed page, and shows in future behaviour that the content has been to some degree internalized. Apart from the people who literally cannot read, I would maintain that the number of *genuinely* reluctant readers is very small indeed. Most boys are quite eager to read about the football match in the *Evening News*, or about their friend who has just been in court. Those interested in motor bikes or hi-fi will happily buy a magazine each week and devour language the technicality of which leaves me in a state of almost complete incomprehension. Almost every teacher who has conducted CSE oral exams will

3

testify to the vast range of printed material of which we are otherwise totally ignorant.

And the girls? Publishers are making fortunes out of our 'reluctant readers'. Most magazines are weekly, and relatively cheap, with a circulation ranging from just over one hundred thousand to over half a million (*Jackie*). A few are monthly, such as *Honey*, *19*, and *Look Now*, and more expensive, but even these have a circulation of around two hundred thousand. The contents pages are similar; interviews with pop stars, reviews of the latest records, fashion articles, and, most important of all, romances. Love stories of a kind to make readers of *People's Friend* blush, to be sure, but fiction nevertheless. For a selective list of magazines currently available, see Appendix A.

Reading is by no means limited to magazines. Books based on current films and television programmes like *Dr Who*, *The Bionic Woman* and even *Poldark* and *The Duchess of Duke Street* sell well (see Appendix B), and some of these books are fairly difficult linguistically. I have written elsewhere about my experiences with a book called *Skinhead* by Richard Allen.[3] My main thesis there was that it is possible to take a badly-written book and use it in such a way as to teach effectively such difficult concepts as authorial stance and different uses of narrative, concepts which are less easily recognised in more complex literature. Five years on the book is still popular, and its seemingly endless string of sequels will, I suspect, forever flourish and abound, as the prayer says, even if learning, by our normal definition, does not. They *are* learning, though, even if we find the content unpalatable.

By selective vision, then, I mean that there is reading which takes place all the time which we do not see, but I think it is part of our job to know that it is going on, and that there is reading going on which we sometimes *choose* not to see. Our pupils are not stupid, and I'm not sure that our pretence does anything to help us gain respect. If we brush off their interests, are they not justified in doing the same to ours?

4 Ephemeral beings

We are all living in a society which is throwaway. This is a fact which many of us deplore, but it is none the less a fact with which we must all come to terms. It is now a number of years since Vance Packard made popular the term 'planned obsolescence',[4] and it has become a facet of modern societies which no one can ignore. Without its reliance on the disposable, modern capitalism as we know it would collapse.[5] Cars could be rust-proofed, but aren't. Nappies are no longer washed, but thrown away. Most bottles are now 'non-returnable', i.e. we have to get rid of them as best we can. Fashions in clothes, entertainment, even hair-styles change, especially amongst the young, with great rapidity. Business depends upon it.

As with material things, so, perhaps, with values. 'Progress' has become a battle cry; success is measured in percentages. We are being told on all sides that we live in an age of change. Michael Marland has called it the age of eclecticism. We are all faced with a baffling range of choices, and the wider the range, the less likely we are to stick to one thing. Why not dabble in as many different things as possible? When applied to values, the implications are doubtless frightening, but that doesn't make them any the less real. If the ephemeral is becoming the very fabric of the lives of those we teach, we can no longer regard it as unimportant. We must be aware of it ourselves, and teach our pupils to be aware of it. This applies as much to their reading habits as anything else. The list in Appendix A shows the most common reading matter of fourth and fifth form secondary pupils. It is compiled from the order book of my local news-agent, and checked against what the pupils themselves say. I am not suggesting for one moment that we should read these every week. What I *am* saying, though, is that we should be well acquainted with the nature of the genre. I would insist on the literary term. It has analyzable characteristics just like any other genre, and good critical work can be produced through a careful analysis.[6]

5 The reluctant teacher?

The problem here, I think, is that much of the work being done by academics has not yet really filtered through to the working teacher. Part of the explanation for this must be the sheer weight of the average teacher's work load, but it is also a result of the four specific problems so far discussed. We ignore at our peril the significance of the sociogram, although its use in inexperienced hands obviously has drawbacks and dangers. We now acknowledge the importance of group work within the classroom, but how often do we extend its use into the reading lesson? Why should every pupil in the class be on the same page at the same time, or even reading the same book? Given a choice of four or five, or even the run of the stock-cupboard, groups will form themselves naturally. Obviously there are immense practical problems, but I believe these can, and must, be overcome, even if pupils are reading largely unsupervised in corridors and spare corners in buildings which were admittedly not designed for such activities. The prerequisites are not as daunting as they might seem; a good relationship (and the element of choice helps here), an up to date worksheet bank on every book in stock (plus an 'all-purpose' worksheet for the pupil who turns up with a book he has bought himself), an efficient record system to prevent popular books from disappearing (preferably a page in the teacher's mark book, or an exercise book with a page for each pupil), and a willingness to trust the pupils to take responsibility for their own work.

Is this just theory? At the time of writing, in my comprehensive school, my fourth form is working like this: four boys are reading *The Contender* by Robert Lipsyte; six girls are reading *The Pearl* by John Steinbeck; one girl is reading *Siege at Robin's Hill* by Christine Dickenson; three girls are reading *There is a Happy Land* by Keith Waterhouse. Other books currently in use in the same class are J. D. Salinger's *Catcher in the Rye*, Thomas Hardy's *Far From the Madding Crowd*, E. R. Braithwaite's *To Sir With Love*, Evan Hunter's *The Blackboard Jungle*, and Shakespeare's *King Lear*, and one girl, having read and worked on three Hardy novels in four months, is reading *Coriolanus*, having asked for more Shakespeare after reading *King Lear*, her first ever experience of Shakespeare! I find it impossible to equate my experience with the widespread feeling that full mixed-ability teaching holds back the bright pupils.

As an example of the increasing interest being shown by academics in working-class and pop culture, one only needs to turn to the contents pages of *Working Papers in Cultural Studies* produced by the Centre for Contemporary Cultural Studies at Birmingham under Stuart Hall. There one finds articles on 'People and culture', 'Football and cultural values',[7] 'Subcultural conflict and working-class community', 'The Motorbike within a subculture group', 'Writing about rock',[8] Women in sport',[9] 'The politics of popular culture',[10] 'Girls and subculture', 'The politics of youth culture', and 'Doing nothing'.[11] More from the 'right', but equally important, are the *Tract* publications, especially number three – 'Towards a people's culture' by Charles Parker,[12] and number four – 'Manipulation and the people' by Fred Inglis.[13]

I think this admittedly non-random selection illustrates my point, that 'culture' must be seen in a much wider framework than that provided by Matthew Arnold or T. S. Eliot:

> I discuss what seem to me to be three important conditions for culture. The first of these is organic (not merely planned but growing) structure, such as will foster the hereditary transmission of culture within a culture; and this requires the persistence of social classes. The second is the necessity that a culture should be analyzable, geographically, into local cultures; this raises the problem of 'regionalism'. The third is the balance of writing and diversity in religion – that is universality of doctrine with particularity of cult and devotion.[14]

This is too narrow a definition. We must be prepared to come to terms with, though not necessarily accept, the importance of the connections between the various elements of pop culture – hair-styles, clothes, entertainment – as well as the importance of group and sub-cultures. It is my argument that it is our very reluctance to do this which puts up a barrier between ourselves and the reluctant reader, and indeed the reluctant pupil. I suspect that in most cases the two are one and the same thing, the result of a reaction to *our* reluctance to understand his way of life.

To summarize, what I am suggesting is that the term reluctant reader is misleading, unless we are also prepared to consider that we as teachers base our judgment on our pupils' ability or reluctance to read 'good' literature. We all too often assume that 'the same only less' is a possible solution to the problem. We are often reluctant to come to terms with the literature they do read, and we tend to regard ephemera as by definition unimportant. Perhaps most telling of all, we don't always feel it is worthwhile even to try to understand the complex world of pop culture in which our pupils live.

Having looked at some of the contributory factors to the existence of the reluctant reader, it seems to me that the approach which has the most practical possibilities is one which abandons the use of the global term. The problem is then seen in terms of the specific child, and specific texts.

The specific child

Every teacher, not just his form master, should have access to a child's educational record, which should be as detailed as possible in terms of as many reading ages at various stages of his development as possible. Reading is not an isolated activity. We should know about his attainment in all subjects, and his attitude to school in general. We should know about his home background, and be aware of his medical record. Much of this material has been traditionally regarded as confidential, but I believe it is essential to have access to it if we are to know the child as fully as possible.

Given all this information, do we accept his attitude as fixed, or keep on trying, if not to alter it, at least to understand it? I know teachers often over-estimate the influence the school environment has in the much wider context of the pupil's life, but we are part of his environment, and should surely do all we can, however little that may be, to make it as rich and satisfying as possible. Presumably we wouldn't be English teachers if we didn't believe that reading could be an important way of achieving this, but we must see this task in the light of Raymond Williams' important and superbly expressed *caveat*:

> To the highly literate observer there is always a temptation to assume that reading plays as large a part in the lives of most people as in his own. But if he compares his own kind of reading with the reading-matter that is most widely distributed, he is not really comparing levels of culture. He is, in fact, comparing what is produced for people to whom reading is a major activity with that produced for people to whom it is, at best, minor. To the degree that he acquires a substantial proportion of his ideas and feelings from what he reads, he will assume, again wrongly, that the ideas and feelings of the majority will be similarly conditioned. But, for good or ill, the majority of people do not yet give reading this importance in their lives. Their ideas and feelings are, to a large extent, still moulded by a wider and more complex pattern of social and family life.[15]

We must find out what he does read. We must read at least some of it so that we can talk positively (this is crucial – to condemn is to reject) and knowledgeably about it.

We must acknowledge the possibility of a specific teacher/child clash, and be prepared to try transference between groups as a possible answer to the problem. Often it isn't, but nothing is lost by the attempt, and potentially at least, success might be achieved.

We must accept that everyone has the right *not* to like certain books. Reading is a personal thing, and we have no right to *impose* our tastes on pupils who perhaps are at their most impressionable age anyway. To be convinced that what is good to us must be good to them is little better than arrogance. As Coleridge said to Poole, 'It is insolent to differ from the public opinion in opinion, if it be only opinion'.

Specific texts

It should be clear from my argument that a very wide range of literature is of crucial importance, since choice of reading matter can only be significant if a genuinely wide range of material is available. This is possible at no extra expense by severely limiting the purchase of full sets for the stock-cupboard. Instead, five or ten copies are adequate if work is organized on guided individual choice. What matters is the number of different titles available, because, as Williams says:

> Nobody can raise anybody else's cultural standard. The most that can be done is to transmit the skills, which are not personal but general human property, and at the same time to give open access to all that has been made and done. You cannot stop a child reading a horror comic, or a man reading a strip newspaper . . . by telling him that it is bad. You can only give him the opportunity of learning what has been generally and commonly learned about reading, and see that he has access to all that is available to be read. In the end, and rightly, his choice will in any case be his own.[16]

The format of the books should also be given careful consideration. There is no doubt in my mind that the reluctant reader prefers paperbacks. As well as having them in the stock-cupboard, each English teacher can have a box of books in his classroom, and school bookshops, once established, make good outlets for cheap, attractive and up to date books.

Cover, layout and quality are all of obvious importance in bringing the book to the pupil's attention, and in making it survive that first suspicious inspection. The cover has perhaps the greatest impact of all on the reluctant reader. It is this, initially, which conditions whether or not a book will be selected for further investigation. Educational publishers could learn from the publishers of such books as *Skinhead*. Of books already available, I think that many of the Macmillan *Topliner* series, and their *Club 75* books for younger pupils, along with the glossy Longman *Imprint* series, offer an immediate appeal.

After the cover comes the 'blurb'. Pupils do read this. If it is well-written, it can act as a powerful *apéritif*. Too often, though, it isn't. Pupils don't want to know what critics have said, or even, at this stage, what else the author has written. Quite simply, they want to know what the story is about.

Most magazines contain pictures. McLuhan tells us that we are getting more visual- and less print-conscious, so perhaps the insertion of pictures in novels is not necessarily a debasement, but an extension. Books for younger children have always contained illustrations and, occasionally, high-quality line drawings, and this feature could surely be extended into books for the secondary age group, and even into their textbooks. I have whetted reluctant appetites by showing them, for example, Quentin Blake's superb illustrations for Carroll's *The Hunting of the Snark* (Folio Society, 1976) and Doré's haunting engravings for Coleridge's *The Rime of the Ancient Mariner* (Dover Publications, 1970). There is no doubt that page after page of small print is daunting to all readers, let alone the reluctant. The stories should be well laid out, preferably with quite a lot of space at the beginning and end of chapters. Cheap, thick paper yellows quickly, and is unpleasant to touch. A book should be pleasing to the touch, and to the eye, as well as to the mind.

There are no gift-wrapped 'solutions' to the problems posed by the reluctant reader. What I am arguing is that if we, as teachers, see the problem, in the context outlined above, as one of putting the right book in the right hands at the right time, rather than as an attempt to bridge a distance between one 'superior' and one 'inferior' culture, then we are much more likely to succeed. I suspect that, with the reluctant reader, presentation is half of the battle. Encouragement, and sheer hard work on the part of the enthusiastic teacher, as opposed to one who shows reluctance, is the other.

References and notes

1 ELIOT, T. S. (1944) 'What is a classic?' in *On Poetry and Poets* Faber
2 ELIOT, T. S. (1951) 'Tradition and the individual talent' in *T. S. Eliot Selected Essays* Faber
3 BARDGETT, K. (1972) '*Skinhead* in the classroom' in *Children's Literature in Education 8*
4 PACKARD, V. (1965) *The Hidden Persuaders* David McKay
5 See TOFFLER, A. (1971) *Future Shock* Pan
6 See BOOTH, W. C. (1961) *The Rhetoric of Fiction* University of Chicago Press
7 SHUTTLEWORTH, A. (1971) 'People and culture' and CRITCHER, C. (1971) 'Football and cultural values' in *Working Papers in Cultural Studies* Centre for Contemporary Cultural Studies, University of Birmingham
8 COHEN, P. (1972) 'Subcultural conflict and working-class community', WILLIS, P. (1972) 'The Motorbike within a subcultural group' and FOWLER, P. (1972) 'Writing about rock' in *Working Papers in Cultural Studies 2* Centre for Contemporary Cultural Studies, University of Birmingham
9 CRITCHER, C. and WILLIS, P. (1974) 'Women in sport' in *Working Papers in Cultural Studies 5* Centre for Contemporary Cultural Studies, University of Birmingham
10 JONES, B. (1974) 'The politics of popular culture' in *Working Papers in Cultural Studies 6* Centre for Contemporary Cultural Studies, University of Birmingham
11 MCROBBIE, A. and Garver, J. (1975) 'Girls and subculture,' CORRIGAN, P. and FRITH, S. (1975) 'The politics of youth culture' and CORRIGAN, P. (1975) 'Doing nothing' in *Working Papers in Cultural Studies 7/8* Centre for Contemporary Cultural Studies, University of Birmingham
12 PARKER, C. (1972) 'Towards a people's culture' in *Tract 3* Cryphon Press
13 INGLIS, F. (1972) 'Manipulation and the people' in *Tract 4* Cryphon Press
14 ELIOT, T. S. (1948) *Notes Towards the Definition of Culture* Faber
15 WILLIAMS, R. (1961) *Culture and Society* Penguin
16 *Op. cit.*

Appendix A

The following is a *selective* list of magazines currently available and being read by the reluctant reader:

Girls	*Boys*
Blue Jeans	Aeromodeller
Diana	Angler
Disc 45	Angler's Mail
Fabulous 208	Autocar
Family Circle	Bike
Good Cooking	Cycling
Jackie	Captain Britain
Leo Sayer	Football Monthly
Look In	Goal
Look Now	Marvel
Love Affair	Motorcyclist Illustrated
Love Story	On Four Wheels
Mates	Roy of the Rovers (Scorcher)
Mirabelle	Shoot
Oh Boy!	Superbike
O.K.	War Picture Library
Pink	Which Car?
Starsky and Hutch	
Supersonic	
Superstar	
Valentine	
Woman	
Woman's Own	

Appendix B

Paperbacks: success stories

What makes a best-selling paperback? What are the magic ingredients for success? We looked at the sales figures for last year from the major paperback houses – a few declined to reveal theirs – and came up with some answers. We list below the 40 top sellers of 1976.

Pan came out easily the number one with *Jaws* by Peter Benchley (70p) – **1,800,000**; in its first year it sold a million. Not far behind came James Herriot's *Vet in Harness* (60p Pan) – **1,280,000**. Frederick Forsyth's *The Dogs of War* (85p Corgi) – **1,000,000**, predictably a winner, will be made into a film later this year. Another film-to-be title was Jack Higgins's *The Eagle Has Landed* (80p Pan), a political thriller about a German attempt to kidnap Churchill, **800,000**. Fontana had a sure-fire seller with Alastair MacLean's *Breakheart Pass* (70p) a Western suspense story – **755,000**. Futura's success also came from a film book, *The Omen* by David Seltzer (60p) – **750,000** and Pan's *One Flew Over the Cuckoo's Nest*

by Ken Kesey (75p) which originally came out in 1973 rather quietly, then with the appearance of the film sold **650,000**. Agatha Christie's posthumous *Postern of Fate* (60p Fontana) – **550,000**. Overall she is still their top-selling author selling some three million books last year. She was followed closely by another Fontana author Desmond Bagley with his thriller *Snow Tiger* (70p) – **520,000**.

Television tie-ins also accounted for many successes: Irwin Shaw's *Rich Man, Poor Man* (£1·25 New English Library) – **522,000** – a kind of American *Buddenbrooks* about two brothers. The combined sales of Futura's two-volume *The Duchess of Duke Street* (both 60p) by Mollie Hardwick came to over **500,000**, a third volume is planned for this summer. Winston Graham's saga of 18th-century Cornish folk *Ross Poldark* (75p Fontana) – **480,000**; the five Poldark volumes, with the undoubted help of the TV series, together sold well over two million copies last year. *All the President's Men* by Bernstein and Woodward (75p Quartet/Futura) – **480,000** – and a film to go with it.

Non-fiction wasn't on the whole a great seller, but Charles Berlitz's *The Bermuda Triangle* (75p Panther) did well – **445,000** – a geographical phenomenon which has been dealt with in several TV documentaries. Catherine Cookson's *The Mallen Girl* (50p Corgi) – **410,000**, followed closely by David Niven's first volume of his autobiography *The Moon's a Balloon* (60p Coronet) – **400,000**. Altogether the book has sold some two and a quarter million copies and Coronet have every right to expect a winner with *Bring on the Empty Horses* published this month. Alex Comfort's *The Joy of Sex* (£1·95 Quartet) tied with another Catherine Cookson novel, *The Invisible Cord* (75p Corgi) – **360,000**. Comfort's book averages 30,000 a month. Almost the only history was Cornelius Ryan's *A Bridge Too Far* (£1·25 Coronet) about the battle of Arnhem – **350,000**.

Emmanuelle by Emmanuelle Arson (60p Mayflower) – **338,000**. And from the same company Len Deighton's *Spy Story* (60p Panther) – **320,000**. Robert Pirsig's cult book *Zen and the Art of Motorcycle Maintenance* (95p Corgi) – **270,000**. Happily the odd classic does appear: Heming-

way's *The Old Man and the Sea* (50p Panther) – **230,000**. James Clavell's epic novel of feudal Japan in the 17th century, *Shōgun* (£1·95 Coronet) tied with James Mitchell's *When the Boat Comes In* (75p Sphere Books) a family tale of survival in the industrial north in the 1920s – **225,000**.

Another film tie-in title which did well even before the film was released here was *Ninety Minutes at Entebbe* by William Stevenson and Uri Dann (85p Corgi) – **220,000**.

Horror stories didn't figure too largely, but James Herbert succeeded with *The Fog* (75p New English Library) – **194,000** – a story about a fog that drives people mad.

Popular science did well with Lyall Watson's *The Romeo Error* (80p Coronet) – **160,000** – a book subtitled 'A matter of life and death'. William Golding's classic *Lord of the Flies* (70p Faber and Faber) – **150,000** – tied with D. W. Lovelace's 1933 success *King Kong* (65p Futura) – which made these figures in the month of December alone, and also with Mervyn Jones's novel *Holding On* (75p Quartet), recently serialised on television. Television was also responsible for the success of *The Goodies Book of Criminal Records* (£1·75 Sphere Books) – **145,000**; and Richard Llewellyn's *How Green Was My Valley* (90p New English Library) is an example of how a television series can revive old sales figures – **144,000**. Faber have a perennial best-seller with their gynaecological guide to life, *Everywoman* by Derek Llewellyn Jones (£1·10) – **100,000**.

Two firms, Penguin and Arrow (Hutchinson) declined to give precise figures, but furnished us with their top titles instead. Penguin had the indefatigable Richard Adams with *Shardik* and *Watership Down* (both 80p Penguin and Puffin), together with a golden oldie, *Animal Farm* by George Orwell (50p).

Arrow had a Douglas Reeman novel, *The Destroyers* (70p) – a naval adventure of the Second World War and, under his pseudonym of Alexander Kent, *Signal – Close Action* (70p) a historical sailing novel set in the 1790s. Under both names this author is a constant best-seller. And Robert Rostand's *The Killer Elite* (65p) – a political thriller, which was made into a film last year. Both of these houses would certainly figure high in the overall lists.

No poetry, no drama, no biography, no art, little history. In fact the successful categories are repetitively limited. The answer to success clearly lies in the hands of a script writer.

Suzanne Hodgart

This article is reproduced with permission from *The Sunday Times Magazine*.

2 Reading fiction - starting where the kids are

Geoff Fox

*Lecturer in Education, School of Education,
Exeter University*

It is said that when the salmon are running to their spawning-grounds up the great rivers of British Columbia, a man can cross from one bank to the other without wetting his feet. The Indians of the North-West Coast, whose own lives took their rhythm in part from the salmon's cycle, believed the fish were a super-natural race who dwelt in vast halls beneath the ocean. There, the Salmon-People took human shape, feasted and danced. When the time came for the run, they dressed in the flesh of the fish to sacrifice themselves for the sake of men. A few were trapped, netted or harpooned; most went on to spawn. As they watched the spent bodies of the parent salmon drift back down the river, the Indians knew that the spirits of the fish were returning to their houses beneath the sea.

According to custom, mothers (and even fathers) of new-born children were discouraged from eating salmon; the presence of a girl entering puberty was believed to be offensive to the fish, and she was forbidden to approach a river; a twin had special power to encourage a bountiful run. Each year, the arrival of the first of the species was honoured by the First Salmon ceremony, which was common to every tribe along the Pacific Coast.

The stories of the salmon (and the bear, the eagle and the deer) were necessary to the Indian; as a separate person, as a member of his community and as a being within the greater order of all creation. The legends provided a framework which could give pattern and unity to the worlds of internal and external experience; a meeting-place where the coherence of the stories offered the hope of coherence in life itself.

The area of play for the young child seems to serve as a similar meeting-place for inner and outer experience.[1] Catherine, aged five, was unlucky enough to suffer a serious eye injury as she played in her back garden. Through two long spells in hospital, she lay flat and still in darkened rooms with her eye bandaged. Whatever terrors she may have known in the ward and in the operating theatre, they were never spoken. She remained cheerful and patient, making the visits of adults far less anguished than they had feared. Nevertheless, inner experience found overt expression when she came home. For weeks after her second stay in hospital, neat rows of dolls, teddy bears and furry cats regularly lay under handkerchief coverlets in Catherine's curtained bedroom, each with a white patch over the right eye.

As Catherine grows up, she may be subject to pressures which work against her instinct to fuse inner and outer experiences. Many schools, mirroring the society they serve, tend to promote and value activity to the exclusion of reflectiveness; a competence in public tasks to the exclusion of a savouring of private learning. In developing the capacity to be objective and in focusing only on the outer world, we find, as Ted Hughes has argued, the inner world 'indescribable, impenetrable, and invisible'. Hughes suggests that the lines of communication between inner and outer worlds in Western culture have become 'disconnected'. This breakdown in communication is no less than the atrophy of the imagination, for the patterning of our experience through the interplay of inner and outer worlds is an essential imaginative activity. The consequences could not be more serious:

> The inner world, separated from the outer world, is a place of demons. The outer world, separated from the inner world, is a place of meaningless objects and machines.[2]

The meeting-place of inner and outer worlds where Catherine contained her eye injury, where the stories of the salmon helped the Indian to give meaning to his life, is then reached through an act of imagination. Without such places to 'play', we may be much the poorer; more brittle, less able to contemplate alternatives in our thoughts and actions as we make less sense of our experience. This is one of the strongest arguments for bringing stories to readers – reluctant or otherwise – for without them we are without one of the most accessible ways of making connections between the inner and outer worlds of our experience.

If we believe story matters, it seems worth trying to determine the nature of the activity of reading in the hope of shaping our work with fiction in schools more appropriately. One way of struggling with the intractable question, 'What actually happens when teenagers read fiction?' is to listen to them talk about books they have read. It is rarely possible to do this in a relaxed way with individual readers in the classroom. Student-teachers on practice usually have a more limited time-table, however, and may even be better able to resist the temptation to 'teach'. It has been useful to consider the findings of a series of studies carried out by student-teachers from the School of Education, Exeter University, each study involving about one hundred third- and fourth-year pupils from secondary schools.

In one study, each student-teacher talked with five children in separate interviews lasting about an hour. The interviewers were guided by a grid of questions which first encouraged the young reader to jot down ideas about the ways in which books had made an impact upon him. These notes, and some further questions, were then used as the basis for conversation. Some responses were brief, though often incisive ('*Jaws* made a deep impression upon me'). Others were more reflective.

Gillian had thoroughly enjoyed Stan Barstow's *Joby*, and her interviewer asked why she had liked the book so much.

Gillian: Well, I don't know really. You feel very sad because Joby's unhappy in parts.
Interviewer: Which part do you think he's unhappiest in?
Gillian: I think when he first hears his mother is going

away. He's really upset by it – all through the book really. (*Long pause.*) My father went away once for a long time – and he had a very big operation. He was away three weeks and I know it made me very nervous – and I got angry ever so easily. In lessons you wander along and you don't think about what you're supposed to be doing. You wonder what's going on but you don't really know. When the phone rings you really jump to answer it. You're terribly afraid.

Gillian seemed to be finding a place between the text of *Joby* and her fears about her father where she set the two experiences alongside each other. The presence of a listener enabled her to make this matching of experience overt: in the usual context of a class of thirty or more, her reaction might well have remained inexplicit (though not without value) not only to Gillian's teacher, but to Gillian herself.

Beverley was described by the English department of her comprehensive school as being a pupil of moderate ability. The list of authors she had read recently emphasised the diversity of much teenage reading: Agatha Christie, Anna Sewell, D. H. Lawrence (*Sons and Lovers*), and a clutch of Enid Blytons and pony books. She was currently absorbed by *Jane Eyre*. Her favourite character was Mr Rochester, whom she saw as:

... tall, dark, gentlemanly. He has a bowler hat and an umbrella. The sort of character that would be willing to take you out for a meal. He wouldn't 'go dutch'. He'd wear a clean pair of socks every day. He wouldn't darn them, he'd throw them out and get a new pair.

The accuracy of Beverley's reading of the text may be dubious; but if we wish to 'start where the kids are', then this is where, thoroughly engaged in her reading, Beverley is.

Bevis, the Victorian pastoral classic by Richard Jefferies, might seem an unlikely book to appeal to a secondary modern reader, again of 'average ability'. John noted:

> *Bevis* influenced me greatly. It altered my whole approach to life. I used to stay indoors and do nothing, but now I want to get out and do something adventurous. It made me feel that if you want to do something, you can.

It is to the unpredictable, idiosyncratic nature of the reactions of Gillian, Beverley and John that we shall return.

The uniqueness of each reader's response was again reflected in a second study. Groups of five third-year pupils were asked to listen to the first chapter of Fay Sampson's *F.67* (Hamish Hamilton, 1975), which describes a trainload of children *en route* for Gatwick Airport. They are being evacuated from the UK because F.67, a substance used to rot down rubbish, is emitting poisonous fumes. They are separated from homes, parents, and pets, without knowledge of where they are being taken, or when they will be reunited with their families. Each child is allowed only one toy, one book, and no items of clothing or luggage which contain plastic.

Before the reading, the pupils were asked to have ready paper and something to write with, although reassured that no testing would follow and that anything they wrote could remain private if they wished. After the chapter had been read to them by the interviewer, they were asked to write down for about ten minutes as much as they could remember of what had passed through their minds as they had listened.

Some responses overlapped in their general themes, especially concerning the listeners' own parents; in their expression and emphasis, they were as diverse as the experiences of the readers. Perhaps the most melancholy reaction was offered by a boy who, despite the preliminary reassurances, could only write:

> **I was thinking of what we were going to do afterwards. I thought we would have to answer questions about the story,**

so I tried to remember in my mind small details like the boy's second name and which school he went to.

Diane wrote:

I thought what it would be like for me to be in their position. Having to leave my mum and future step-dad, and our little cat, Midge. And the problem I would have had if I had to leave my things behind. The thought of being shut in that train, the noise and being crammed. And that thing which would terrify me most would be the thought of not knowing where I would be going and if I would ever see my mum and future step-dad again.

Janet saw F.67 affecting her own neighbourhood:

My mum and dad. My brother. My cat. I felt sick. 1940. A green gas enveloping Burnthouse Lane. My brother's school cap. A dream I once had about Burnthouse Lane falling down and I saw my teddy bear on a table in the front room. Trees falling down. My brother can look very sad and poorly.

Mark listed his reactions:

Despair. Loss. The living dead. Bones. Goodbye for a century. Adapting. Living alone. Strangers.

Pam's notes reflected a way of moving wholly into a story which, perhaps ironically, adults trained in English Studies rarely retain:

I hate hearing any stories that tell of suffering to children. It really hits home. It reminds me of a couple of months ago when I couldn't sleep for fear of never waking up again or thinking I had a terrible disease like cancer. It reminds me of the love I have for my parents and how I couldn't bear to

ever leave them like that, and it makes me want to cry to
think of my brother and sister who died so close to me and
my parents, they're gone, gone for ever, away from us, who
knows where, they're dead. Death, that's the root of all fears.

Various elements in the process of reading can be recognised
in these studies; others, no less important, may be beyond the
conscious grasp of the readers.[3]

1　The reader may realise that his own experience and
　　feelings are common to others. Gillian found in Joby a
　　boy whose fears matched her own anxieties for a sick
　　parent.

2　Throughout a novel, the reader may be evaluating, and
　　in that sense testing out, possible ways of behaving as he
　　watches fictional characters. He may make such evalua-
　　tions of the behaviour (or aspects of the behaviour) not
　　only of characters he admires, but also those whom he
　　dislikes or even fears. James Bond, for reasons which are
　　not too elusive, was still a figure much envied by adoles-
　　cent boys in the studies, though no girls confessed to
　　admiration for him.

3　A reader may gain a specific insight into his own feelings
　　and behaviour. One American boy, whilst reading
　　David Copperfield, smiled and said:

> I'm not sure I should smile. I've just discovered I'm
> Mr Micawber – in the making, that is.[4]

4　As a reader stands within the world of his book, he may
　　find a better perspective in viewing his own involved and
　　often incoherent experience. To take the clearest ex-
　　ample: the charge of escapism has often been levelled
　　against readers with a strong taste for fantasy. Tolkien,
　　and others, have replied that to choose for a while a
　　universe patterned with its own sanity may be a renewing
　　escape from the confusing to the rational.

5   Fiction may provide another means of gaining informa-
    tion which determines future thought and action; it
    encourages the consideration of alternatives. Jane had
    read David Rook's *The Belstone Fox.*

> After I read it, I gave up hunting because I began to
> see fox-hunting in a new way. I saw it from the fox's
> point of view. It would be very unpleasant to run for
> miles being chased by hounds and people on
> horseback. I haven't been fox-hunting since, and I
> don't think I will again.

Two other dimensions of the reading activity are worth dis-
tinguishing, though it is less possible to give evidence for their
existence since they stand beyond the conscious recall of the
reader.

6   It seems safe to believe that reading fiction is a powerful
    means of developing the reader's own use of language.
7   Fiction may provide a means of developing a sense that
    the power of a reported experience comes from the form
    in which it is related as much as from the experience
    itself. In short, much of our reaction depends upon the
    way a story is told, the way in which order is imposed
    upon incoherence.[5]

Each of these aspects of the process of reading might then be
seen as a way of making meaning, either of the outer life in the
past, present, and even the future; or of our inner lives, often in
relation to the outer life. However, private reading is not the
only way in which story may enable us to make such meanings.
Listening to stories in the classroom or at home might work
similarly though not identically, for the process is different. The
teller may control the process more; he will modify his words and
facial expressions as he watches the reactions of his audience.
The responses of the other listeners in turn will modify that of

the individual. Watching stories on the screen involves a process which is different in degree if not in kind from reading stories. One image is replaced rapidly by another. There can be less time for reflection. This is not to argue the superiority of private reading over other forms of receiving stories; merely to suggest differences in the processes. The most important consequence of the differences seems to be that in private reading what we ourselves bring to the story has the greatest opportunity of shaping the experience free from external interventions. The implications for our teaching are numerous.

To match the varied reading experiences of the thirty or more pupils in a class, we need to leave space in our teaching for each reader's unique reaction, and to confirm its importance to him. Whether the pupils are juniors or school-leavers, any hopes of encouraging a lifelong habit of reading depend upon an abundant and various supply of reading material which is immediately available in the classroom. The material may be paperback or hardback; novels, short stories, plays or poetry; magazines, newspapers or comics; fiction or non-fiction. It may be bought with school funds, on long loan from the library services, lent by members of the class. The quality of the reading may be equally diverse. Certainly there should be demanding as well as light reading.

The first tactic in dispelling 'reluctance' is to make free reading amongst this wide provision of material a frequent activity of the class. This is only to reaffirm the findings of researchers from Jenkinson (1940)[6] to Whitehead (1975);[7] the class library is the most effective means of encouraging reading. Since the reader's response is both unique and unpredictable, this is surely the only way of ensuring that we 'start where the kids are'. In establishing a reading 'climate' through time regularly spent in free reading, a teacher need have no feelings of guilt that he is 'not teaching'. He will in fact be busy in helping with choices of books and, when possible, in listening. Beverley, having finished her conversation about *Jane Eyre* and Mr Rochester in particular, said to her interviewer:

I've learned a lot. I've never talked about books before –
just written in English. I now feel more about the books,
through explaining to you.

To advocate free and regular reading of this kind is not to
propose that there is no place for all-class reading. Short stories
read aloud in a class where the climate of reading is already
valued are a shared pleasure in themselves, and on occasion may
allow public exploration of concerns whose personal relevance
to an individual need never be revealed in the discussion. Some
stories, especially those which have elements of myth, encourage
both a private and a corporate response. A touchstone for our
class- or group-teaching of fiction might be this: have we
provided a space – perhaps through writing, or talking with a
partner in an exploratory way – which might encourage each
reader's response? The examples of the written reactions to
F.67 quoted earlier in this chapter show how readers have used
such a space. If his responses are immersed in the opinions of the
teacher or other children, or immediately buried beneath work-
sheets or comprehension questions, it is very probable that a
reader will be increasingly reluctant to value reading as an
activity.

It may well be that further work with other pupils in writing,
collage, painting or model-making, with tape-recorders, in
retelling a story in dramatic terms, or simply in talking together,
will modify and refine the personal response to a text. Enjoyment
and a desire to read closely may well be encouraged, not smoth-
ered. The kind of direction which is surely less justifiable is that
which uses novels and stories as spring-boards: a story involving
a child's relationship with his grandparents is reduced to a question on a worksheet demanding, 'What can we do to help Old
People?'; Henry Treece's Viking adventures herald only an
integrated studies project. The fact that many children saw
fiction as a preface to other work may lie behind one of the most
sobering facts to emerge from the student-teachers' enquiries:
only one out of every ten readers from the twenty schools in-

volved said that books 'done in class' were amongst their favourites.

'Starting where the kids are' presupposes, then, teaching which begins with a readiness to acknowledge what a reader brings to a book as well as the text on the page. Resources are not unlimited, however, and some choice in the provision of books may be necessary. Teachers sometimes argue that they teach or recommend only fiction which they enjoy themselves. The discussion in this chapter of the idiosyncratic nature of reading emphasises the fallacy of such an argument. If I dislike science fiction and am uninterested in sports stories, where can I start with the diffident readers in my class who are addicted to *Dr Who* and *Match of the Day*? Literary judgments as well as personal tastes are involved. What delights the experienced reader (subtlety of characterisation, the ironies which inform a plot, the detailed description of a landscape) may deter a less assured reader. What an English teacher might judge to be hack writing may be no cliché to a reluctant reader. For him, the ideas and their expression may be new; if they are familiar, they may serve to draw him farther into the book by the reassurance that he is on manageable, recognised ground.

The field of literature for young readers is a curious one. Adults write the books; publish, sell, buy, review and award prizes to the books. There are areas of the field where it sometimes seems a child has never walked. The publication of books with reluctant readers in mind stemmed from the needs of those who could hardly avoid children, since they saw them all day in classrooms. Aidan Chambers, the founding editor of the Topliner series for reluctant readers, is surely right in his belief that 'wide, voracious, indiscriminate reading is the base soil from which discrimination and taste eventually grow'[8]. Initially, it was in such a belief that the series for reluctant readers were published. As the series have proliferated, discrimination becomes more necessary; but in this, as in the methods used to foster the enjoyment of fiction in schools, it seems essential to begin with the personal reactions of young readers to the books they read.

References and notes

1 For a full discussion of this theme see BRITTON, J. (1971) 'The role of fantasy' first published in *English in Education* 5, 3 and reprinted in MEEK, M. *et al* (1977) *The Cool Web* Bodley Head
2 HUGHES, E. (1976) 'Myth and education' in G. Fox (ed) *Writers, Critics and Children* Heinemann Educational Books
3 Each of these categories merits an essay in its own right. Perhaps the most useful background reading for an attempted description of the reading activity is HARDING, D. W. (1962) 'Psychological processes in the reading of fiction' first published in the *British Journal of Aesthetics* 2, 2 and reprinted in MEEK, M. *et al* (1977) *The Cool Web* Bodley Head
4 Quoted in HARTLEY, H. W. (1951) 'Developing personality through books' *English Journal* 34, 10, 198–204
5 See LESSER, S. O. (1960) *Fiction and the Unconscious* Peter Owen Ltd
6 JENKINSON, A. J. (1940) *What Do Boys and Girls Read?* Methuen
7 WHITEHEAD, F. *et al* (1975) 'Children's reading interests' *Schools Council Working Paper 52* Evans/Methuen Educational
8 CHAMBERS, A. (1973) *Introducing Books to Children* Heinemann Educational Books

3   A reluctant literature?

Robert Leeson
*Literary and Children's Editor of the Morning Star
and author of six books for young people*

If reluctant readers present a problem to the professionals – to teachers, librarians, educationists – what thoughts can the writer offer? What can a writer do about it? What should a writer do, if the word 'should' can be used without the writer drawing in both horns and retreating into the protective shell? Fiction writers who do approach the question of the reluctant reader do so with – well – reluctance. Aidan Chambers in his highly interesting work on the subject devotes a whole chapter to the 'reluctant writer', in fact.[1] And like reluctant readers, reluctant writers are a mixed bunch.

There are writers who find it distressing to consider readers at all, believing they write 'only for themselves' as fervently as they hope no one will take them at their word. There are those who believe that if you deliberately write for any category of reader you are doomed to formula writing and the old muse will fly out of the window. And yet others see reluctance among young readers as a problem much larger than it is within their individual ability to solve or even grapple with. And to write for reluctant teenagers who, it would seem, have been steadily put off books for the past thirteen years at least, by home, school or other influences, is asking a lot of the average writer, who is no hero.

Even Thor, in the old legend, when invited to drain the drinking horn, might well have hesitated a bit if he had been told, 'By the way, Comrade, we've dipped the other end in the sea'. Any writer, considering the majority of young people who do not read, or read without enthusiasm, or only when obliged to, may

29

well say, 'I'll settle for the difficult, writing for the volunteers, and leave the impossible, writing for the conscripts, alone.' The impossible, even in the most optimistic of outlooks, takes a little longer than the difficult, and at first sight the rewards, material or spiritual, for attempting the impossible are neither close at hand nor attractive.

The reluctant reader, after all, is part of the wider problem of education which in its turn bears a heavy burden from the past. Only now are the schools teaching teenage pupils whose parents, in the majority, are themselves the product of the expanded education of post-war years. The teenage pupils of the 1960s and early 1970s were in most cases the sons and daughters of parents who were educated under the old pre-1944 educational set-up, leaving school at fourteen.

The majority of these pupils had grown up in homes where there were no books. But what is more, the parents had gone to schools in which, under the old regime, books – to read for pleasure – were very thin on the ground. My own recollection of the pre-1944 days, which can be compared with that of others of my generation, is that we were taught to read, write and add up by hard-working teachers, whether we were the majority destined to leave at fourteen to go into farm, shipyard or munitions factory, or the minority (two to three per cent in my school) destined to go by scholarship to a grammar school to the age of sixteen. when family circumstances forced another halt in education.

To be able to read was one thing – and as I discovered during my army service quite a few were unable to fill in even simple forms – but to read with skill and pleasure was another matter. How did one practise? There was a library box which came round to school now and then, with one copy of each title, even the most popular ones. No school library of course. Our parents, outside the school, had to rely on the once-weekly library van. The first-ever branch library in the place where I was born was built in – 1976.

In school, few books. At home none, and not much room to

read either. In my own home, where education was our religion, four of us did our homework in shifts round the same kitchen table. These kind of conditions are not so common these days, of course, though as teachers know, they are still to be found.

The burden of the past then is immense, and still affects the present generation, even after two raisings of the school leaving age, the increased expenditure on education, the growth of school libraries and the work of a new generation of teachers and school librarians. The present financial stringency has come just at a time when one might begin to see some of the effects of all the post-war effort.

Yet change there has been. The sales of children's books have mounted year by year since the last war, and during the past decade the sales of paperbacks for children have rocketed. Today there are several thousand school bookshops to reinforce the school libraries in making books available more easily – books as things to keep, not to hand in after use every day. And outside the schools organised parents have begun to make their influence felt. The work of the Federation of Children's Book Groups in popularizing books, particularly among the younger children, is another factor not to be underestimated.

The combined effect of these changes, working upon fresh generations of pupil-parent-pupils, will eventually gather momentum. I firmly believe that if the education cuts and other physical obstacles can be overcome, then we shall indeed see progress of a kind very rewarding to the teachers and others who have struggled with the problem so long. Someone, Goethe I think, suggests that a question or problem presents itself with greatest force and clarity when the means of answering or tackling it is to hand.

But any change, as it takes place, will involve the writers. I won't say 'must', because it sounds like 'should'. Change will involve the writers because it will call forth new writing. To expect reluctant readers to be won without new writing is to miss a vital aspect of the meaning of reluctance, a resistance to the inside as well as the outside of the book.

There are perhaps 30,000 titles in print for young people of all ages, from first-reading to new-adult stage. If overcoming reluctance were a matter only of transforming the potential reader, there should be variety enough to hand in most schools. But, dislike of the book as a book, or even indifference to it, ingrained as it is in many people for very weighty historical reasons, is not the main point. No one should be under illusions even about those who appear never to have opened a book. They often have a shrewd idea of what is inside. Their attitude is often backed by experiment, albeit unsystematic. They may simply be confirming their own prejudices by a little carefully chosen research, something not unknown among readers. On the other hand they may be looking genuinely, if not very hopefully, for something – perhaps for credibility, simple direct contact with their own existence, insight into a life and world which change around them so bewilderingly at times, an insight that will make the strange, familiar and the ordinary, exciting. They are looking, and often enough they are just not finding.

I think I know a little of what is in the reluctant young reader's mind. In the course of sixteen years of work as a literary editor I have had nearly 15,000 books for children and young people pass through my hands. Some were non-fiction of course, and I am concerned here largely with fiction. Out of those thousands of books, I can say that my reviewers (parents, teachers and young readers themselves) and I found some 3–4,000 works of fiction good enough to recommend to our readers and their children, or 2–300 every year – much less than a third of those considered and no more than ten to fifteen per cent of the total published annually. Some of the rejected books were of the cheap-and-nasty kind. But most were well produced, nicely bound, sometimes well illustrated, typical products of a children's book trade in a country proud of its production standards. They were not badly written by conventional standards either. Many of the authors were clearly seized of the best principles of literary creativity, educated and articulate people with wide vocabularies. Thinking back over them and trying to fix on a common inadequacy, I can only say that they lacked bite, they lacked grip, they were bloodless, they were cosy and nice in a way which has earned those words a bad name. Still, some of them found their way on to library shelves and may be there to this day. As more than one school librarian has told me, even highly praised and award-winning books may so sit undisturbed by even keen readers or, if disturbed, put back fairly soon. The silent or monosyllabic critique of the young consumer, reluctant or otherwise, is a harsh one.

The special feature of this branch of reading is that the consumer is not the buyer – except in the case of paperbacks, often bought by children. On the positive side this means that in the schools the young reader or would-be reader can be given a wider range of choice than would be sustained by their instant likes and dislikes. Sustaining this variety through the years as the reader matures and the reluctant reader hopefully becomes less reluctant, the teacher and librarian can ensure that doors on benefit and pleasure are not entirely closed.

There is a negative side however to the separation of buyer from consumer: the market can operate in disregard of the consumer to a marked extent, and in disregard of the potential consumer to an alarming degree. The relative independence of the children's book world from the full pressure of consumer demand and resistance has nourished a 'high' critical and evaluative attitude which I think has helped disorientate the writer.

A seemingly logical train of argument has been built up, going something like this: books for young people include some of the finest written; the classics of this kind appeal not only to children but to adults; a truly good book for children is also a good book for adults; therefore a really good book may be recognised by its appeal to adults, and a book which only young people like is a bad book. Thus the appeal of a book to children is no criterion by which to judge quality, and to write a good book for children you must satisfy adult demands. On no account must you surrender your judgment to the tastes and demands of the young readership. One writer was recently mortified to be told that her books might be popular with young people but they were not 'literature'.

In this 'high' critique (and its influence on writers for young people cannot be doubted) there is little room for the willing consumer. How much room is there for the reluctant reader? None at all. Publishers of books aimed at the reluctant reader often spare themselves and their writers pain by not putting them out for review.

What we have to contend with, it seems, is not simply a reluctant readership, but a reluctant literature. There have been successes over the past twenty-five years in producing books of merit which appeal to a wide range of young readers. This cannot be disputed. But the successes owe more, I would argue, to the change in the environment in which literature is consumed in schools and libraries than to the development of critical standards, which have tended to set their face against the consumer.

I believe that this change in environment will, in the long run, increase the number of young book readers or lovers. But they will not shift over to 'our side' in some form of unconditional surrender. The shift will affect both sides and the literature *will* change ('will have to' sounds too much like 'should').

If the shift really takes place it will be of immense importance to writers, inspiring existing ones and discovering new ones – perhaps from among the reluctant readers of yesteryear. Above all though, and most important, I hope that this change will do something to restore to writers a birthright surrendered over the past 500 years: true, living contact with readers or audience.

To go back to the reluctant readers as I have met them in homes, youth groups, schools, they are each one of them individuals, with very varied personalities. Yet I have noticed one thing common to all: they are reluctant to read a story, yet I have never known any of them refuse to listen to one. This has significance for the author.

As writers at our desks, in contact by telephone with our editors, we can and do survive if eighty per cent of potential readers refuse to open our books. But if we were telling our story direct to an audience of any age and discovered that three-quarters of them were not listening, we should pack up and go home, unless we found some crafty way of swapping stories or even changing the course of a story in mid-stream. As writers we may write 'for ourselves'. As story-tellers we know the customer is always right. We have to know because the customer is there in front of us. As writers we can subsist on the mechanical reproduction of our words and their distribution to an unseen percentage of the audience without actually setting eyes on a single one of them. Our story-tellers' birthright, then, has been sold for a fairly thin bowl of gruel, never mind a mess of pottage.

Yet if writers are anything they are story-tellers. Humans are born, hunt or grow food, and tell stories about how it was done. If story-telling is not the oldest profession, it is one of the oldest. If one were to set the tale, to judge from the subject-matter of the oldest myths and legends, among the organised hunters of earlier inter-glacial periods, then the story may be 30,000 years old – far older than writing and far, far older than printing. To put it another way, if story telling began on New Year's Day, manuscript recording and storage began on the first week in November and printing began on Boxing Day. Our year's evolutionary cycle being thus completed, however, we cannot all renew ourselves by putting on skins and rushing off into the forest lands. But a profit and loss account at the year end would do no harm.

The story-tellers' audience was all the people within earshot at a given moment, regardless of age or condition. Chaucer's pilgrims came from all walks of life; each had different tastes in stories; but each listened to all. Stories were restricted in length. All story-tellers must have noticed how, after twenty minutes, eyes glaze and heads turn. If you had a long tale you told it in portions, complete in themselves and with bait to bring back the eager listener next time.

While the audience was in his grip the story-teller could extemporise, expanding old tales, with due respect to his listeners' memory and prejudices. He could moralise, no aesthete rising from beside the fire to object when he proclaimed 'That was a *good* king'. He could politicise, at his own risk, 'bearers of tales to the discredit of the kings' ministers' being liable for punishment. If he lost his grip on his audience, he could not say he was born ahead of his time, nor that his audience was reluctant. The artist in him may (or may not) have rebelled when met with demands for yet another tale of Jack, Robin, Sir Gawain or Sir Bevis. The professional in him sought protection from the Ministrels' Gild against competition from 'rude husbandmen and artificers'. And the story-teller might have to contend with what I believe the Germans called 'mit-dichtung des Hörers' – a form of audience participation which enriched or held back the story according to your view.

Printing and the book changed all these things. They gave the writer length, breadth, endless freedom to write. If the reader tired, the book did not. It could be laid aside, picked up again. It gave the writer an audience with fewer physical limits. His readers might sit a thousand miles away. In place of the localised, ever-present audience was a network of kindred spirits, separated from one another; and separated from the rest of the population by their ability to read the symbols into which the living story was transcribed, and by their possession of the book which contained them.

That printing made possible the possession and accumulation of knowledge beyond previous dreams, is an old story. So also is the popular movement to possess that treasure store. But printing did create two social gulfs: one between those who could read and those who could not – a gulf still not entirely bridged – and another between the teller of the tale and its hearer. Between writer and reader (each in their private world) came publisher, printer, bookseller and finally critic and interpreter. In compensation for the loss of contact with his audience, the writer was offered greater creative scope – a real benefit – and the status of special person destined to be more highly valued by fewer and fewer – a very dubious benefit.

36

An added complexity inevitable in the development of printing was specialization, not least the separating out of a literature designed for the growing but still dependent members of the community, the young: a literature in which the beneficial and informative and the pleasurable were deemed irreconcilable and in which the old stock of verbal myth and legend, where all virtues were irregularly mixed, was relegated to a subordinate position.

The young population too were divided into those who could read and those who could not, those who owned books and those who did not; or those who possessed worthy books specially written for them and those who made do with cheaper, lurid, mangled versions of old legends and folk tales, with tales of new rogues and revellers grafted on to the dying stock, forerunners of the comics of today.

For one part of society, books of serious creative intent were deemed from the earliest age part of a civilized way of life. For the rest of society, the majority, books were above all for two sorts of people: those who wanted to get on in the world, now seemingly in the possession of people who had books, the key to knowledge; and those who wanted to change that world. A century of 'universal' education has only just begun to alter this basic social division. A veteran Communist organiser told me how during the 1930s, when travelling in unfamiliar areas, he could find the family he wanted to visit by looking down the terraced streets for the window which gave a sight of a small shelf of Penguin and Left Book Club editions.

I have argued that these divisions or their shadows are with us to this day. The profit and loss account of the social changes to which the invention of printing contributed is still not properly drawn after 500 years. Only with the full accomplishment of universal education does the invention come near to realising its full potential. The gains for the writer and writing during these 500 years – the fusing of the many story streams in the river of the novel, with its seemingly endless possibilities for character and theme exploration – are well enough known. Not so well known are the losses, the gradual distancing of the writer from the reader and, in the latest period, the parallel separation in creativity, of technical mastery and psychological mastery from the art of the graspable story. The highly qualified writer, at odds with the public, even seeing virtue in alienation from people at large, is a familiar, but not a pretty, sight.

That a literature subject to such developments should have its quota of reluctant readers is hardly surprising. And those developments have certainly affected literature for children and young people. The effect has been less than in the area of adult literature though, mainly because of the opportunities for direct contact between writer and audience. This audience can be defined; it is localized in schools; it is willing to receive the writer as story-teller and craftsman; and once its attention is won it is more ready to change, to look afresh at life, than the rest of society. It has a great urge to know about life, if possible in advance of stumbling over its obstacles. The fact that teenagers 'tire' of books they once took pleasure in may sometimes be the result of an unconscious feeling that the books are holding them back when they want to feel their way forward. Through the story the young reader can experience life vicariously, positively, even painlessly, and yet be subtly changed by an experience at one remove.

Direct contact with such an audience is something each writer in this field should experience and be changed by. In such direct contact, one cannot ask the willing and the reluctant to line up on either side of the room, nor does one even inquire privately which is which. One tells the tale, or one talks to these real people, watching faces and eyes with care for the first sign of contact dying. No Scheherezade's head, about to be parted from its body talks more willingly. If only every writer had written large above his desk 'Remember Scheherezade' I dare swear there would be fewer reluctant readers.

Such contact may be good for the audience. It is certainly good for the writer. One simple thing it has taught me, for example, is to make each chapter no longer than can be listened to without the eyes wandering. I have followed this rule, whether writing straightforward comic stories of modern life, or working with the greater complexities of a historical trilogy set in the sixteenth and seventeenth centuries. I should like each chapter to stand being taken out separately and read aloud to its corresponding age group, irrespective of whether they are believers or unbelievers.

It is not unknown for writers when working to read aloud what they have written, if only to themselves, and strike out that which sounds false: the verbal tricks and fancies; the artificialities that look one way on the page and sound another when spoken. The choice of words is influenced, the proportion of verbs to adjectives even. No writing submitted to the reading test is ever the same again.

Writing consciously for an audience which groups the non-reader with the reader is not to be confused with what I call the 'convoy fallacy' – the idea that writing for reluctant readers means travelling at the speed of the slowest or seeking the lowest common denominator. Writing with the reluctant reader in mind is not writing for dull wits or slow thinkers. Nor is economy in the choice of words a device for addressing people with small vocabularies. It is rather the method of addressing the widest range of hearers at the same time, with a precision which gives unmistakeable signs of the author's intention (his style), a simplicity which leads to the utmost clarity. This is achieved by selecting and fining down, not by multiplying and proliferating.

Another lesson to be learned via the reluctant readers comes from studying the television they watch. Television may have drawn some young people away from the book, but I would guess it has drawn more towards it. And I would assert that in the better television adventures and serials they get what they do not get in a deal of modern writing – immediacy of involvement and identification, quick grasp of essential action, with no time lost in setting the scene, one picture often being well worth a thousand words. Television as competitor is perhaps the enemy of one sort of 'fine writing': that which loves description for its own sake; that, I think, which makes the potential reader close the book and put it away. He is in good literary company, for nearly 2,000 years ago, Apuleius in *The Golden Ass* made merciless fun of the 'rosy-fingered dawn' specialists. Get on with it, was his message. Get on with it, is the message of the square screen. Get on with it, is the plea of the reluctant reader.

'They don't want to read about character, all they want is action', complained one teacher at a conference I attended. Her 'they' were not city children at a large comprehensive, but pupils at a fairly expensive private school. I could appreciate her frustration, but they were right. The division she was making, and which a lot of writing also makes, is a false one. Character can be described in a static way – and, if you are an addict, writers who take a deal of time over it give you a great deal of pleasure. But above all character emerges in action. The word 'motive' comes from the same root as the word 'motion'. What *moved* you to do that? Mindless action, action for its own sake, does appeal, but this does not mean it is *all* the reluctant reader wants or will accept. A deal of poor writing directed towards reluctant readers is poor because of this assumption that action and character are lower and higher elements in literature. The most thrilling stories are those in which each turn of the action flows from the relation between the characters and their destinies. One action does not follow the other, but arises from it, and the final consummation of the interaction of thought and deed comes like a hammer-blow. You do not have to be a connoisseur to like a good plot, nor for that matter, scorn a bad one to do so.

Speed in movement, logic in event and action, economy in description, care in constructing dialogue so that it may carry some of the burden of narrative, these are all lessons learnt both from story-telling and from the television, both of which look to a universal audience. 'Even the Queen has to watch the box', said someone. For it is a universal readership you are aiming at, not reluctant or un-reluctant readers. You are maximizing your audience, and direction and simplicity are part of the strength you must impart to your story so that it will stand the pressures the diversity of your hearers will put on it.

Simplicity, let's assert once more, is not the cutting down of the fabric of a story, like the making over of a suit, to fit a lower intellectual capacity, any more than seeking the terseness of the fundamental Anglo-Saxon roots of English, is a concession to the imagined low vocabularies of a reluctant audience.

No final clue can be gained as to the vocabulary of a person, young or old, simply by hearing them speak or even by studying what they read. Many writers are inarticulate almost to the point of incoherence; their speech is no guide to the complexity of their thought. This is true too of their potential readers. The writer is in any case not addressing the outward personalities of his readers, but their inward selves. Once past the barriers of speech and convention, the inhibitions of class and environment, and writer and reader are in open country.

Speech is the very devil for giving the wrong impression. Still many writers for young people believe they can give colour to character by a crude phonetic rendering of sounds alleged to come from people's mouths. Cockneys, north-country people, west-country folk, are represented by some mangled approximation of their speech, much as BBC-trained actors before the last war used to put on 'an authentic accent' according to the need of the play. Today's drama draws on a great variety of actors who can truly represent the speech of people from all parts and all walks of life. But still in books the tired old tricks, the 'yus' and the 'bah gum', are trotted out. Superior people from an area roughly marked by the Home Counties, however, do not have accents, they speak the word as printed. There can be no more unconscious yet arrogant assertion of superiority on the part of the writer.

For me this reducing of whole social groups of people on the printed page is a relic of the past, related to the crass efforts which used to be made in some schools to 'cure' pupils of their local accent. One of my most vivid memories of school is of having a stand-up argument with a teacher over this policy – if one can dignify this kind of snobbery with such a name.

Acutely conscious as a school pupil of being spoken down to, of being instantly under-valued at the sound of my voice, I was less directly but inescapably aware of this discrimination expressed on the printed page. It is, I believe, a not uncommon experience for people growing up in this way. If writers (and editors) do not realise that young readers are aware, however vaguely, when they and their like are being belittled in books, then I would urge them to reflect on this most carefully.

In this and in other ways, in too many children's books, ordinary people still appear not as subjects but as objects. A multitude of associations aggravates the alienation of this kind of writing from potential readers. They sense it is not of them, about them, or for them.

It is my conviction that the restricted social setting and attitude of many books for young people contribute to the general 'bloodlessness' – lack of vigour and completeness – I wrote of earlier. To take an example: in this kind of book the villains have been reduced in status, from the men of power they were in the old folk-tale, to the level of petty crooks, an obsession of suburbia which appears time and again in children's books. Indeed in many such books the petty crook is the only guise in which the working-class majority may appear. One critic recently complained that some modern social-realist writers were trying to reverse the trend, with political intent, by making the villains for example, property developers, outwitted by determined children. The intention of course is no more political than the objection. But the property developer as character at least regains some of the weight and power of the old villain and is a good deal more real in the lives of most children than the cloth-capped rogue trapped by Janet and John whilst making off with Aunt Matilda's antiques.

I am arguing that the narrow social range of many books for young people is one reason for their narrow appeal. This is challenged by those who argue that children of less favoured backgrounds 'do not want to read about themselves – they want to escape in a book'. The assumption here is that such children are so deprived that they place no more value on their own existence than does the aforesaid observer.

All young people like to take on the form of a proxy hero or heroine and thus escape into realms of fantasy, whether they are reading books or watching the 'telly'. And they all like to directly identify with realistic, contemporary, non-fantasy characters, thus passing through the airlock between the here-and-now world and that of the imagination. That the majority of children should be obliged to make two flights of fancy, one to get into the character of more favoured young people, and a second to get into the inner, imagined world of the book, is asking that these children should *surrender their own identity* in order to enter the book-world. Not more than a certain number are prepared to do it.

The idea that 'less fortunate' readers do not see their own back yards as suitable launching pads for flights into the imagination is just another aspect of the restricted image presented by many books. The expression of the full range of social experience in literature is essential not only for it to appeal to those young people hitherto unregarded, but also to provide the vigour and body needed to appeal to reluctant readers from all social levels.

This is a touchy subject. Some critics, having endured without harm a century and more of mediocre 'drawing-room stories' now pronounce themselves, after perhaps a decade, tired of reading 'mediocre kitchen-sink stories'. Behind this rapid critical fatigue in the face of the new social realism, is the unspoken and traditional assumption that life actually begins in the drawing-room and that the kitchen is simply a mechanism for ensuring the continuance of that life. There is therefore no more need to study the kitchen than to take the watch apart to find out the time.

To move away from such assumptions and the literary conventions that go with them requires a conscious effort from writers and editors. Conscious efforts sometimes produce self-conscious writing, or as one academic put it 'selfconscious . . . social engineering'[2]. The writer who consciously identifies with the majority of young people outside the charmed circle of literary convention, with working-class or, say, immigrant children,

43

and who wishes to appeal directly to them, will often enough want to change the set-up which physically discriminates against them. This is why a deal of new writing aimed at reluctant readers breathes a spirit of social conscience and is preoccupied with social problems. Paradoxically, it may thus not appeal to the very young readers to whom it was so warmly offered.

This is a new sort of literature and generalizations are difficult. But I think the weaknesses are not those of principle but of practice and they will be overcome in time. If social-realist novels do not succeed as literary works in their own right, or, more crucially, in their appeal to the chosen audience, it may be because the stories are formed from two parts not sufficiently fused together: the one is the life of the young people portrayed, often sympathetically and accurately; the other is the analysis of the social problem affecting them which is seen from the writer's point of view. Most difficult of all is to see the social scene through the eyes of the young people concerned. It is no good your having a clear view of a social situation if your character doesn't know what you're talking about, or doesn't see it your way. Nor is it any good nudging your character in the right direction.

One of the most difficult aspects of the writing of one of my own books, *The Third Class Genie* (Collins, Armada Lions, 1975), was deciding what went on inside the head of my hero Alec who lived in a northern town where housing and immigration were two intertwined issues. Until I knew exactly how they affected him personally, and not simply the sociologically average citizen of the town, then the story could not move. As writers, we often come upon social problems as they affect millions. But they are in fact the sum of millions of personal problems and lives. Realistic writing gives individuality to the millions and universality to the individual.

But how do young people see life? One can ask, and listen, or one can be more devious. I have a collection of stories, based on my own boyhood and first working years. When I have an audience I tell them a story appropriate to their age range and watch or listen for signs or recognition or bafflement, identification or rejection, laughter in expected or unexpected places. After each telling the stories are changed (one story I published was changed radically after pupils in a school had pulled it to pieces). It is not a matter of changing the reality to suit the audience, but through the influence of that audience gaining a fresh insight into the way I now see the life I once lived. In this way I gain some reference point for the way they see their lives as they pass through those same years of transition I once experienced.

Fundamentally, my audiences are very much as I was, though the world has changed, offering more opportunities with the one hand, more menaces with the other; a world with more ladders to climb up and more holes to fall down than the one I knew. They know more, they see more than I ever did, but they are no whit less vulnerable in relation to today's changes and chances. They need, as I did, a way of looking ahead, of time-travelling into life, of gaining as much experience by proxy as they can before they have to test it for themselves, learning the strokes somewhat before going irrevocably into the water.

Books, with their personal message, the opportunity they provide for reflection, for coming back to, for re-living and brooding over, ought to be the best aid to growing up for every young person. And if a majority of growing human beings does not feel the stimulus, the discovery, the comfort in books, then the inadequacy is ours, not theirs.

References
1   CHAMBERS, A. (1969) *The Reluctant Reader* Pergamon Press
2   MANN, P. H. (1974) in a speech: 'Why should children read?' at the Children's Bookselling Conference, 4 September

4 The development of the teenage novel

Sheila Ray
Lecturer, Department of Librarianship,
Birmingham Polytechnic

What most people mean by 'the teenage novel' is a new kind of book which has come into existence in this country since 1960. Essentially, it is a book published by the children's book department or the educational department of a publishing house, consciously intended for older children of twelve or thirteen upwards. This article tries to explain why the teenage novel emerged in Britain in the 1960s and how it has developed since.

The teenage novel before 1960
Few things appear suddenly without warning; although this article is concerned mainly with what has happened in Britain since 1960, the roots of the teenage novel can be found in nineteenth-century books by such authors as Charlotte Yonge, Louisa Alcott and Susan Coolidge, which are concerned with young people growing up, falling in love and having children of their own. *Little Women*, published in 1868, and its sequels may quite fairly be looked upon as the ancestors of today's teenage novels and some of the same elements are found in them – the problems caused by relationships with the opposite sex, by poverty and war, adjusting to a difficult employer (remember Aunt March), and the sadness of death. In view of the universality of its themes, it is not surprising that *Little Women* has survived for over a hundred years. The incident of Meg and the length of silk on which she spends the housekeeping money in *Good Wives*, has an exact parallel in Honor Arundel's *The Two Sisters*, published in 1968, in which the newly married

46

Maura spends the housekeeping money on a pair of fashion boots.

American writers for older children, of whom Louisa Alcott and Susan Coolidge were only the first, have a long history of popularity amongst British readers and the United States may be said to be the home of the modern teenage novel. The landmark book in the United States seems to have been Maureen Daly's *Seventeenth Summer*, published in 1942, but M. Rankin, in research published in 1940, commented on the great popularity, amongst girls in their early teens, of the Sue Barton books by Helen Dore Boylston, which had first appeared in the 1930s and which heralded a new kind of fiction (careers for girls) in the United States in that decade.[1]

The pattern established in the United States was soon followed by British writers and publishers. The fact that in 1948 the Library Association awarded the Carnegie Medal to Richard Armstrong's *Sea Change*, a book about a boy going to sea with the merchant navy for the first time, and in 1950 to Elfrida Vipont's *The Lark on the Wing*, which told of the hardships faced by the heroine at the start of her career as a singer, shows that attempts were being made to give the adolescent the opportunity to experience through his reading some of the possibilities which lie ahead.

In the early 1950s a number of British publishers made a conscious effort to provide 'career novels'. Pam Hawken's *Air Hostess Ann* (Bodley Head, 1952), Lorna Lewis's *Hotel Doorway* (OUP, 1953), and Louise Cochrane's *Social Work for Jill* (Chatto and Windus, 1954) were fairly typical examples of the genre. The pages of *The Junior Bookshelf* of the period reflect how rapidly the situation changed. In 1952 it was said that 'librarians are crying out for career books', in March 1954 *The Junior Bookshelf* carried a classified list of career stories, and by November of the same year career books were said to be 'flooding the market'. Although these provided useful information about the qualifications and training needed for specific careers, they were read mainly for the story and were, therefore, most popular if the heroine was involved in one of the so-called glamorous careers and there was a strong element of romance, with a husband as well as a career in sight by the end of the book. The smaller number of stories featuring heroes and appropriate male careers, such as C. H. Doherty's *Brian Decides on Building* (Chatto and Windus), were less popular and seldom left the library shelves.

However, until the 1960s, books for young people rarely dealt in any depth with aspects of adult life other than careers. Most authors, when writing for the young, treated relationships between people fairly superficially, if at all. Parents, if not dismissed from the action on the first page by death, illness or business, tended to be puppet characters, doing and saying the things demanded of them by the action. Sexual relationships were virtually ignored, unless an engagement, a wedding or a new baby was announced. The coyness, or innocence, demonstrated by writers for teenage girls in the period between 1910 and 1950 is quite extraordinary and often unintentionally humorous; writers for boys usually avoided such topics.

During the 1950s a few books appeared in which personal relationships were more deeply explored and the change which affected children's books generally after 1960 can be traced back to the work of such writers as Geoffrey Trease and Monica Edwards. Geoffrey Trease's five Bannermere books, published between 1949 and 1956, have a contemporary setting, the mother is divorced, and the developing relationships between the boy and girl characters are realistically portrayed. Monica Edwards is the author of a long series of books about two sets of characters – the Romney Marsh families and the Punchbowl Farm family. The early books were above-average holiday adventure stories with a strong animal interest, very typical of the period at which they were written. In *No Going Back* (1960) the characters become more aware of their sexual differences, and emotional relationships, with all the implications including the effect on other members of the peer group, are allowed to develop.

However, until after 1960 there was little in books published for young people to make the adult wonder about their 'suitability'. Secondary school libraries and the new teenage sections which began to appear in public libraries from the middle of the 1950s onwards relied heavily on children's books, the career novels and certain selected adult novels. The care with which public librarians and teachers selected adult fiction for teenagers is reflected in the booklists of the period where certain books are scrupulously noted with the suggestion that they should be read by the librarian before being placed on the open shelves.

The emergence of the teenage novel in the 1960s

In the period since 1960 young people have become more sophisticated, more aware of the world around them, more subject to commercial and social pressures than any previous generation, and subjects hitherto taboo are now openly discussed with them and amongst them. It soon became clear that neither flooding the market with career stories nor treating personal relationships in a little more depth against a realistic background would meet the demands and needs of young readers.

Those concerned with the reading of young people were aware of these facts, which were given added urgency because, even before the raising of the statutory school leaving age, more young people were staying at school for longer. It seemed appropriate to include relevant themes in books for this age group and it also seemed that these books would have to be specially written so that the themes could be explored at a level which could be understood by those who were still emotionally immature and whose literary experience was limited.

In the early 1960s too there was growing concern amongst teachers and librarians about the fact that many teenagers did not apparently read much fiction and that children's use of both school libraries and public libraries declined, as far as recreational reading was concerned, as soon as they reached their teens. At the conferences which were organized for librarians, teachers and youth leaders, the reasons why this happened were discussed and the view was frequently expressed that the right kind of books, if only they could be written and published, would go a long way towards solving the problem. Adults working with adolescents and books were increasingly aware that there was a gap between books for children and books for adults and that even if some adolescents could cross the bridge satisfactorily, there were many others who could not.

One of the first writers to make an attempt to write specifically for teenagers was Josephine Kamm. In *Young Mother*, published in 1965, she dealt with a topic – a sixteen-year-old schoolgirl's unmarried motherhood – which would previously have been considered quite unsuitable in a book produced by the children's department of a publishing house. Today, *Young Mother* seems innocuous and rather dated, but its publication and that of the author's *Out of Step* (1962), the story of the friendship between a white girl and a black boy, marked a significant shift in the attitude towards themes which were considered appropriate in books for teenagers.

The most striking change that has occurred since 1960 is in the topics which are now mentioned and discussed in teenage novels. In 1969 Geoffrey Trease was able to comment that the child had been liberated:

> He sees people talking without embarrassment about their illegitimate babies, drug-habits, abortions, mental break-downs and sexual difficulties ... I do not mean that all these themes should, or are likely to, become the material for children's stories.[2]

By 1977 attitudes have changed still further and all these subjects have now been dealt with in books for teenagers.

A number of publishers met the demand for books especially for teenagers by developing new series. The first of these was the Peacock series, which Penguin launched in 1962. This series remained small in terms of the number of titles and seemed to lack a coherent policy or sense of purpose, perhaps because it appeared before the British teenage novel had firmly established itself. Early in 1977, therefore, Penguin introduced the 'new'

Peacock series, which consists of 'first-class contemporary fiction' such as Lynne Reid Banks' *One More River* and Graham Greene's *Stamboul Train*, and 'original non-fiction', as well as books written for teenagers such as Julius Lester's *The Basketball Game*. The series is designed to meet the needs of fifteen to seventeen-year-olds 'in search of good reading material who have yet to find their way into the range of Penguin books available'. A few of the early Peacock titles have been retained and the new series offers the fluent teenage reader books to bridge the gap between Puffins and Penguins and reflects the publisher's continuing belief in the need for a special provision for teenagers.

The second series to appear was Pyramids, first published by Heinemann in 1967. Unlike the original Peacock series, which consisted cf paperback reprints of books already published in hardback, the Pyramid series is a hardback series of specially written stories of approximately 27,000 words, designed to appeal to the less fluent, less experienced teenage reader. There are now over forty titles. Two of the first titles were *Marle* and *Cycle Smash* by Aidan Chambers, a teacher, writer and critic, who has played a major part in the development of attitudes towards teenage fiction over the last decade. In *The Reluctant Reader*,[3] published in 1969, he set out what he saw as the desirable elements in teenage fiction, making a passionate defence of this new kind of writing and arguing that if only relevant titles could be identified, or written if necessary, then the reluctant teenager would read.

In 1968 the first eight titles were published in the Topliner series, of which Aidan Chambers is the general editor. Originally published jointly by Pan and Macmillan, the series is now published by Macmillan Education. Aimed primarily at the reluctant teenage reader, the series includes, for example, short, straightforward love stories, thrillers and collections of ghost stories, as well as one or two more demanding novels such as Paul Zindel's *The Pigman*. Many of the books have been specially written for the series and their popularity has borne out Aidan Chambers' assertion that if only authors could be found who could write the books on themes that teenagers wanted to read about, then the reluctance to read would be overcome. A recent development has been the introduction of Topliner Redstars, a series of novels more demanding than the average Topliner and designed to bridge the gap between Topliners and the world of adult fiction.

A number of the titles included in Topliner Redstars, such as William Corlett's *The Gate of Eden* and *Return to the Gate* and J. M. Couper's *Looking for a Wave*, were first published in the Bodley Head Books for New Adults series, the fourth of the series especially designed for teenagers to appear during the 1960s. This is a hardback series which has played an important part in influencing the provision of books for adolescent readers by publishing the work of such writers as Paul Zindel, Peggy Woodford and Lynne Reid Banks. The Books for New Adults series originally made few concessions to the reluctant reader, although obviously some titles were easier to read than others. More recently a number of less demanding books such as Janet Green's *The Six* and Barry Pointon s *Cave* have been added, thus widening the series' appeal.

The 1970s have seen a number of further developments in the provision of books for teenagers. The success of the Topliner series has led two other educational publishers to launch similar series. The Nelson Getaway series resembles Topliners both in appearance and in the type of stories that it offers. Longman's Knockouts, on the other hand, provide a wider range of stories, graded at five different levels, thus catering for the poor as well as the reluctant reader.

Another development, resulting from the increasing concern with standards of literacy among all age groups, has been an expansion in the provision of books for under-achieving readers. This expansion began in the 1960s, but for many years this area of publishing remained the poor relation and little attention seems to have been paid to the presentation or quality of the books being published. Recently, however, a number of new series have been established, while longer established series have assumed more attractive formats, so that teenagers with poor reading ability are now catered for by series of the quality of Club 75 and Rockets (Macmillan), Solos (Hart-Davis), Inner Ring Hipsters (Benn) and Spirals (Hutchinson). An annotated list of series for the under-achieving reader will be found on page 147.

The change in appearance has been evident too in the Topliner and Pyramid series. Topliners, with their paperback format, have always looked attractive, but even in this series the early covers now have a rather old-fashioned look. Wisely, the publishers have up-dated the covers as the books have been reprinted, thus ensuring continuing impact. The most recent Pyramids have glossy, photographic jackets, which are much more appealing than the combination of line drawings and geometric design which decorated the dust jackets of the early titles. Another development has been the increased use of illustrations. The Longman Knockouts series has made use of photographs, while the books in the Checkers (Evans) and Rockets series, for example, contain black-and-white line drawings designed to make them appear less daunting to the reluctant reader.

Although the mention of series is a convenient way of providing a chronology for the development of teenage fiction, many similar books have appeared which fall outside the series. During the period since 1960 books which are for children rather than for teenagers have also changed. The emotional aspects of relationships between the young and adults, and between members of the opposite sex are now considered even in books which would be regarded primarily as books for the under twelves – in the work of Nina Bawden and Helen Cresswell, for example – though here the relationships do not loom very large and the subtleties may often go unnoticed by the child reader. Two of Geoffrey Trease's historical novels, written thirty years apart, conveniently demonstrate the change which has taken place in writing for young people. In *Cue for Treason* (1940), the reader is told on the last page that Kit and Peter will eventually marry but their actions and thoughts throughout the book have given no hint of this at all. In *Popinjay Stairs* (1970), the two central characters, Denzil and Deborah, are older than Peter and Kit, and their relationship, culminating in marriage, is shown developing through the book, alongside the action.

Some features of teenage fiction

Many of the books written for teenagers or adopted by them since 1960 have certain features in common. An essential quality, if the book is to have a wide appeal, is a strong story-line. The development of the literary novel in the twentieth century, as a result of which story has become often a secondary consideration, is perhaps another reason for the growth of a special literature for young people. To attract a large teenage readership a novel must have a plot which moves forward at a good pace, creating suspense and holding the interest in a way which makes the reader want to go on reading. This basic requirement is one of the reasons for the potential far-reaching success of many of the books written for older children. The adult reader in search of a good story may well find the required qualities in the K. M. Peyton Flambard's trilogy, for example.

Another feature common to teenage novels is the inclusion of a character or characters with whom the reader can identify. Often the central characters are young themselves and look at the problems and experience of adolescence from the inside. Occasionally, especially in the case of a straightforward adventure story, the central characters may be adults, but even here this is quite unusual. The typical teenage novel allows the reader to gain experience vicariously through identification with characters not very different from himself, who are involved in situations not far removed from his own experience or which he may anticipate meeting in the future.

The setting must be relevant, although it does not necessarily have to be contemporary, and the distancing factor involved in placing the story in a historical period, in a science fiction future or in a foreign country can, in fact, be an advantage. Setting a story in the past enables the author to look at the problems of growing up, of questioning society and its institutions and attitudes in a more rounded context and with the possibility of suggesting solutions. John Christopher, on the other hand, in a book such as *The Guardians*, uses the science fiction future as a device in which to debate for the young reader some of the dilemmas of contemporary society.

Style is, of course, important. Stories need to be presented in language which is meaningful without being absurd or incomprehensible. Some of the books which have tried to reflect too closely current teenage vocabulary have been dated almost on publication and have been allowed to go quickly out of print. The most successful books have been those using a straightforward narrative style, with little or no dateable slang, or telling the story in the first person, adopting an off-hand humorous style which invites the confidence and involvement of the reader.

Most important of all, if it is to appeal to teenagers, a book requires a theme which they find relevant. Overall, of course, the theme is 'growing up' with all the related experiences and problems; teenage novel after teenage novel shows the hero or heroine coming to terms with himself or herself, learning through experience, and thus provides a measure against which the reader can test his own experience.

One recurring theme is the search for identity and for a positive role to replace uncertainty and insecurity. In Joan Tate's *Sam and Me*, for example, Jo has to learn that she must overcome her feeling of insecurity and make a positive contribution to the relationship with Sam if it is to survive. John Rowe Townsend's central character in *The Intruder* is a boy who feels that his identity has been taken over by an older man with the same name, but he learns to fight back and to make his own niche in society.

An important part of the growing up process is the developing awareness of relationships with other people – with the opposite sex, with parents, with other adults and with members of the same sex. Relationships with members of the opposite sex are undoubtedly a major preoccupation with many teenagers and this fact is reflected in most of the teenage novels. One of the first titles to appear in Peacocks in 1962 was Beverly Cleary's *Fifteen* and this has remained one of the most successful and popular titles, regularly finding a new audience as girls reach the age of twelve or thirteen. Although the adult observer might suppose that this book is by now somewhat dated, it seems to share the qualities of some earlier American girls' books and still strikes a chord in the heart of the girl who comes across it at precisely the right moment in her development. The story covers a year in the life of an American teenager when she meets and goes out with her first boy-friend – who could resist the opening sentence, 'Today I'm going to meet a boy, Jane Purdy told herself, as she walked up Blossom Street toward her baby-sitting job.'? It is the kind of book which the reader grows through, as she sympathizes with Jane who wishes to appear sophisticated, does get her boy, but has to cope with parents who still regard her as a child. One of the reasons why it has remained so popular is perhaps because there are so few books like it. Some of the books about Polly Devenish by Rodie Sudbery, *Rich and Famous and Bad*, *Warts And All* and *Ducks and Drakes*, have the same mixture of charm, truth and humour, and some girls will get the same kind of rewarding enjoyment from Winifred Cawley's *Gran at Coalgate*, the winner of the 1975 Guardian Award, but this last is a much more demanding book in a less attractive format and is therefore in danger of being missed or overlooked. Lynne Reid Banks' *My Darling Villain* also shows the heroine progressing from the stage when she becomes aware of the fact that some of her peer group have boy-friends, through her own involvement with a boy, to the establishment of a stable relationship. The comparison of this last book with *Fifteen* shows how much even the telling of a fairly unsophisticated romance between two young people has changed in fifteen years.

Peggy Woodford's *Please Don't Go* is a sympathetic study of a girl who falls in love with an older man – a not uncommon experience amongst teenage girls – but in this and other books which portray a similar situation the girl is seen to grow through this experience and to settle in a more satisfying relationship with a boy nearer to her own age. These books and many others are concerned with relationships between the two sexes, but at a fairly innocent level.

However, as society's attitude towards sex has changed, so teenage novels have appeared dealing more openly with subjects such as pregnancy and abortion. Josephine Kamm's *Young Mother* was published at a time when abortion was still illegal. In Gunnel Beckman's *Mia* (1974) the heroine is shown full of doubt and despair considering all the possibilities open to her and visiting the local library to look up all about abortion, and the reader shares her relief when it turns out to have been a false alarm.

While some adults might be shocked at the topics which are now covered in teenage fiction, they might also take comfort from the picture which is presented to the reader. When the central characters are shown to be having sexual relations outside marriage, they are usually shown to be discussing the need for, and taking, precautions, and the solution of abortion is not regarded as right nor shown to be an insignificant experience. In *My Darling, My Hamburger* the beautiful Liz, having had her expectations of marriage dashed, undergoes an unpleasant abortion and fades from the story; Maggie, who at the beginning of the story is seen as plain and gauche, following in Liz's wake, emerges as the successful character, maturing, 'going from one year to the next feeling slightly less ridiculous', making satisfactory relationships with boys and graduating from high school. It is, in fact, despite its outspoken qualities, a very moral story.

A large number of books, while admitting the existence of extra-marital sex, tend to draw a veil at the vital moment. Jill Chaney, for example, in *Mottram Park*, responds to some extent to teenagers' curiosity about what really does happen in the sexual experience, but Sheila and Gary's first experience of sex is a failure and this is perhaps, if unconsciously, a warning to the young reader. There is certainly little suggestion in teenage novels that one could or should indulge in carefree sex and that such an experience would be rewarding with no disastrous results. In this respect, at least, teenage novels support the general establishment view, although the fact that extra-marital sex is mentioned at all is a major step forward. The second of Julius Lester's *Two Love Stories*, *Catskill Morning*, set in an American summer camp, handles the situation explicitly but delicately. Emily, sixteen, is attracted to one of the camp counsellors, Mark, who in turn is attracted to her. The book also gives a very good picture of the difference between the male and the female in love – Emily willingly gives up her ballet practice so that they can be together, but Mark cannot give up his need to be alone in the mountains; the story captures exactly the feeling of a young person experiencing a deep sexual relationship for the first time.

Catskill Morning is a short novel but *Mottram Park* has the space to describe the boy-girl relationship against a background of family relationships and this rounded presentation is typical of many teenage novels. Other books make the family relationships the dominant theme. The failing of Honor Arundel's *A Family Failing* is the habit of celebrating when anything special happens in the Douglas family, but this doesn't prevent the family falling apart when father becomes redundant just as mother becomes a successful TV personality. Honor Arundel not only captures in her dialogue the give and take of family life, the bickering and the friction, but also conveys the desirability of family support even from a family which is being torn apart by tensions. Bobby in Alison Prince's *The Doubting Kind* has worse problems: her mother is a neurotic alcoholic in constant conflict with her husband. The problems are heightened in contrast with the rather old-fashioned school problems experienced by Bobby and her friend Fanny; the need to wear hats and to have the proper equipment for school activities seem minor irritations against the tragic background, but they are irritations which young people at school may well experience for themselves.

The problems of steprelationships are also examined in teenage novels since it is at the adolescent stage that conflict is most likely

58

to arise between stepdaughter and stepmother or between stepson and stepfather. Reginald Maddock's *Sell-Out* shows both relationships when Danny's mother marries Lorna's father. Danny resents being replaced as the man of the house while Lorna resents the implied criticism and certain replacement of her housekeeping skills. Sometimes the advent of a stepparent leads the central character into petty crime or the drug scene and the discovery by the central character that he or she is adopted may well have the same result, or at least be the prelude to a period of uncertainty and unhappiness. It may seem unfortunate that the books which deal with these less usual parental relationships seem to emphasise the difficulties, but if everything were perfect there would be no conflict around which to build the story and the eventual reconciliation. Where stepparents or adoption do not provide a catalyst for the action, they tend to go unnoticed.

Another relationship that is explored in a number of books is that between the young and the old. Mia, in Gunnel Beckman's *The Loneliness of Mia*, forms a close relationship with her grandmother, following her parents' separation and the break-up of her affair with her boyfriend Jan. In Paul Zindel's *The Pigman*, John and Lorraine become involved with the elderly Mr Pignati who gives them the freedom of his house, which they then abuse, unable to appreciate that he is as capable of being hurt as they are. Paul, in Susan Price's *Home From Home*, finds in his friendship with old Mrs Marshall compensation for his small stature, his uncomfortable, untidy and noisy home and the lack of communication with his parents. At her house he finds an outlet for his artistic skills and becomes so involved with the old lady that he truants from school. This eventually leads to his mother's discovery of the relationship and the promise of a better understanding in the future. In both these books the reader is given a stimulus to reflect on the loneliness of old age and the need for community support.

Experiences such as the death of a friend or a parent, and serious illness are now brought naturally into teenage fiction in

59

a way that did not happen before 1960. One of the first books in which the central character is shown to die was Jean MacGibbon's *Liz*, published in 1966. David Rees in *Storm Surge* (1975) brings the reader even closer to this situation, while Mary in *Please Don't Go*, having grown through her love for an older man, has to face up to the death of the boy with whom she has formed a real, satisfying relationship. Jane in Honor Arundel's *The Girl in the Opposite Bed* goes into hospital for an appendix operation and comes face to face with death for the first time when the woman in the next bed dies, and with serious illness when she talks to a girl suffering from cancer. Her experiences in hospital help her to develop a more adult attitude to life, to think less about herself and more about other people.

Another subject on which there have been several books, but which would have been considered quite unsuitable twenty years ago, is drugs. In S. E. Hinton's *That Was Then, This Is Now* Bryon, the central character, comes up against drug taking and rejects the idea of taking drugs himself. He also has to make up his mind to betray his adopted brother, Mark, of whom he is very fond but whom he discovers to be a drug pedlar. The treatment of the drug theme in this book is rather different from that found in most of the books which had originated in this country before its appearance. British writers, such as Madeleine Duke in *The Sugar Cube Trap*, had tended to take up a rather tentative, establishment attitude, using the taking of drugs as a catalyst to the main action of the story. However, John Branfield in *The Scillies Trip* (1975) makes the drugtaker's sister the central character; the drug scene is accepted, described and shown as undesirable without hysteria.

John Donovan's *I'll Get There, It Better Be Worth the Trip*, an American book published here in 1970, is one of the few teenage novels which touches on homosexuality although so discreetly that many young people might miss the point. Luke in *Quintin's Man* by David Rees discovers that a boy he had much admired at school is gay and is fascinated by the fact, but the hero's involvement is as an observer. As in the case of explicit descriptions of sex, British writers tend, rightly perhaps, to take the conventional viewpoint and if homosexual relationships are mentioned the central character with whom the reader identifies is not involved. The shortage of teenage books on this theme is noticeable even in the USA.[4]

To many insecure and frustrated teenagers running away from home may seem to be the answer. This experience too is described in teenage novels but is usually shown to be unsatisfactory and even more full of problems – lack of money, the need for food and shelter – than the situation from which it seemed an escape. Dick in Jill Chaney's *The Buttercup Field* is so upset by the reactions to his gift to Jessica of an expensive brooch, that he sees escape to the anonymity of London as the only solution. Graham in John Rowe Townsend's *Goodnight, Prof. Love*, involved with a girl, and Jerzy in Joan Tate's *The Long Road Home*, condemned as he sees it to the dull prospect of a lifelong career in accountancy, both run away. It is significant that although Dick and Jerzy, at least, fall on their feet, they all return home and come to terms with their situations.

In view of the fact that the teenage novel first manifested itself in the career story, it is surprising that the work experience has not been better covered by later books. Although some of the career novels which were originally published at the end of the 1950s have been up-dated and are still in print, something more than this is required. Two recent novels which point the way are Martin Ballard's *Dockie*, and William Mayne's *The Incline*, but both these books are set in the past. Prudence Andrew's *Goodbye to the Rat* gives an excellent picture of the problems of the academically unqualified in finding a job but says comparatively little about the problems which may arise once the job is found.

Although books published for young people in Britain began to reflect the multiracial society soon after it became established fact, the emphasis amongst writers for the young has been on integration and a minimization of the problems, so that although characters of West Indian or Asian origin are included, care is taken to present them in a favourable light. In *Out Of Step* by

Josephine Kamm (1962), Betty and Bob apparently accept that they cannot marry and it is perhaps typical of the British writers' approach to race and colour that no book published for teenagers by a British writer since this has been any more outspoken on this particular topic. British readers have to turn to American sources for books like Kristin Hunter's *The Soul Brothers and Sister Lou*, set in a black ghetto in a northern city, and Julius Lester's *Two Love Stories*, in which the first story, *Basketball Game*, is concerned with the friendship of a black boy and a white girl in a southern American town. Where the problems are thoroughly aired, as they are in these two books, it may be that a distancing factor is desirable. For those teenagers who can cope with them, some of Rosemary Sutcliff's historical novels such as *Blood Feud* concern themselves with slavery and mixed marriages and may have more emotional force than a novel struggling for contemporary authenticity.

Once girls have passed beyond the stage of liking to read about tomboys, they seem to prefer their heroines to adopt a fairly conventional female role, with marriage and domesticity as the ultimate aim. Liz in Paul Zindel's *My Darling, My Hamburger* is not untypical in the fact that she is quite reconciled to her unwanted pregnancy when she believes that Sean is going to marry her and visualizes herself working as long as she can, only so that Sean can still go to college; she willingly accepts the stereotyped secondary role. Emma Sheriden in Louise Fitzhugh's *Nobody's Family Is Going To Change*, another American book published here six years later, expresses a very different attitude. Emma is black, wants to be a lawyer and has to come to terms with the fact that you can't persuade your family to change its views. However, the book also makes the point that acceptance doesn't mean that you personally have to give up your ambition, but this book is still unusual enough to have won The Other Award for its non-stereotyped portrayal of society.

Questions of colour and race, the role of women and class are all explored by Robert Leeson in his linked trilogy of books set in England and the American colonies in the sixteenth and seventeenth centuries, another example of the use of the past to illuminate the present. These books, '*Maroon Boy*, *Bess* and *The White Horse*, express a strong feeling for truth and social justice; Matthew Moreton has modern, liberal attitudes towards slavery in '*Maroon Boy*, while Bess, his sister, is thoroughly emancipated and racially tolerant to the extent that she forms a liaison with a Cimaroon chief. Their son returns to fight on the side of the Parliamentarians in the English Civil War.

No article of this length can hope to discuss the full range of themes on which teenage novels have been written. From those which have been mentioned, however, it can be seen that the novels published for young people in the late 1970s are vastly different, both in content and in style of presentation, from the first teenage novels of the early 1960s. Yet, despite their outspoken coverage of a wide range of controversial topics, the majority of teenage novels tend to reinforce conventional and establishment attitudes. While it is impossible to predict exactly how the teenage novel will develop over the next decade, one possibility would seem to be an increase in the number of books in which the stories suggest alternative viewpoints and offer a challenge to the stereotyped views so often presented to teenagers by the mass media.

References and notes

1 RANKIN, M. (1944) 'Children's interest in library books of fiction' *Contributions to Education* 906 New York: Bureau of Publications, Teachers College, Columbia University
2 TREASE, G. (1969) 'Children's reading is changing' *Books and Bookmen* 14, 8
3 CHAMBERS, A. (1969) *The Reluctant Reader* Pergamon Press
4 See HANCKEL, F. and CUNNINGHAM, J. (1976) 'Can young gays find happiness in YA books' *Wilson Library Bulletin* 50, 7

Appendix
Reading list

The following list identifies the titles mentioned in the text; it is *not* a list of recommended books. OP indicates that the book is currently out of print. Where both hardback and paperback editions are available, the details of the hardback edition are given first.

ALCOTT, L. M. (1868) *Little Women* Many editions available e.g. Blackie, Chosen Books; Penguin, Puffin
ANDREW, P. (1976) *Goodbye to the Rat* Heinemann, Pyramid
ARMSTRONG, R. (1948) *Sea Change* OP
ARUNDEL, H. (1972) *A Family Failing* Hamish Hamilton
ARUNDEL, H. (1970) *The Girl in the Opposite Bed* Hamish Hamilton; Macmillan Education, Topliner
ARUNDEL, H. (1968) *The Two Sisters* Heinemann, Pyramid
BALLARD, M. (1972) *Dockie* Longman, Young Books; Collins, Armada Lion
BANKS, L. R. (1977) *My Darling Villain* Bodley Head, Books for New Adults
BANKS, L. R. (1973) *One More River* Vallentine Mitchell; Penguin, Peacock
BECKMAN, G. (1975) *The Loneliness of Mia* Bodley Head, Books for New Adults; Longman, Knockouts
BECKMAN, G. (1974) *Mia* Bodley Head, Books for New Adults; Longman, Knockouts
BOYLSTON, H. D. (1939) *Sue Barton: Student Nurse* Brockhampton, Knight Books
BRANFIELD, J. (1975) *The Scillies Trip* Gollancz
CAWLEY, W. (1974) *Gran at Coalgate* Oxford University Press
CHAMBERS, A. (1967) *Cycle Smash* Heinemann, Pyramid
CHAMBERS, A. (1968) *Marle* Heinemann, Pyramid
CHANEY, J. (1976) *The Buttercup Field* Dobson
CHANEY, J. (1971) *Mottram Park* Dobson
CHRISTOPHER, J. (1970) *The Guardians* Hamish Hamilton; Penguin, Puffin

CLEARY, B. (1962) *Fifteen* Penguin, Puffin

COCHRANE, L. (1954) *Social Work for Jill* OP

CORLETT, W. (1974) *The Gate of Eden* Hamish Hamilton; Macmillan Education, Topliner Redstar

CORLETT, W. (1975) *Return to the Gate* Hamish Hamilton; Macmillan Education, Topliner Redstar

COUPER, J. M. (1973) *Looking for a Wave* Bodley Head, Books for New Adults; Macmillan Education, Topliner Redstar

DALY, M. (1942) *Seventeenth Summer* Available in UK only through Scholastic Publications

DOHERTY, C. H. (1960) *Brian Decides on Building* OP

DONOVAN, J. (1970) *I'll Get There, It Better Be Worth the Trip* OP

DUKE, M. (1969) *The Sugar Cube Trap* White Lion Publications

EDWARDS, M. (1960) *No Going Back* OP

FITZHUGH, L. (1976) *Nobody's Family Is Going To Change* Gollancz

GREEN, J. (1976) *The Six* Bodley Head, Books for New Adults; Longman, Knockouts

GREENE, G. (1948) *Stamboul Train* Heinemann; Penguin, Peacock

HAWKEN, P. (1952) *Air Hostess Ann* OP

HINTON, S. E. (1971) *That Was Then, This Is Now* Gollancz; Collins, Armada Lion

HUNTER, K. (1971) *The Soul Brothers and Sister Lou* Macdonald

KAMM, J. (1962) *Out Of Step* Brockhampton

KAMM, J. (1965) *Young Mother* Brockhampton

LEESON, R. (1975) *Bess* Collins

LEESON, R. (1974) *'Maroon Boy* Collins

LEESON, R. (1977) *The White Horse* Collins

LESTER, J. (1974) *Two Love Stories* Penguin, Kestrel; the first story, *Basketball Game*, is also available from Penguin, Peacock

LEWIS, L. (1953) *Hotel Doorway* OP

MACGIBBON, J. (1966) *Liz* Heinemann

MADDOCK, R. (1969) *Sell-Out* Collins; Macmillan Education, Topliner

MAYNE, W. (1972) *The Incline* Hamish Hamilton; Penguin, Puffin

PEYTON, K. M. (1967) *Flambards* Oxford University Press, Penguin, Puffin

POINTON, B. (1976) *Cave* Bodley Head, Books for New Adults

PRICE, S. (1977) *Home From Home* Faber

PRINCE, A. (1975) *The Doubting Kind* Methuen

REES, D. (1976) *Quintin's Man* Dobson

REES, D. (1975) *Storm Surge* Lutterworth

SUDBERY, R. (1975) *Ducks and Drakes* Deutsch

SUDBERY, R. (1970) *Rich and Famous and Bad* Deutsch; Transworld, Carousel

SUDBERY, R. (1972) *Warts And All* Deutsch; Transworld, Carousel

SUTCLIFF, R. (1976) *Blood Feud* Oxford University Press

TATE, J. (1971) *The Long Road Home* Heinemann, Pyramid

TATE, J. (1968) *Sam and Me* Macmillan Education, Topliner

TOWNSEND, J. R. (1970) *Goodnight, Prof. Love* Oxford University Press; Penguin, Peacock

TOWNSEND, J. R. (1969) *The Intruder* Oxford University Press; Penguin, Peacock

TREASE, G. (1940) *Cue for Treason* Blackwell; Penguin, Puffin

TREASE, G. (1949) *No Boats on Bannermere* Heinemann

TREASE, G. (1973) *Popinjay Stairs* Macmillan; Penguin, Puffin

VIPONT, E. (1950) *The Lark on the Wing* Oxford University Press

WOODFORD, P. (1972) *Please Don't Go* Bodley Head, Books for New Adults

ZINDEL, P. (1970) *My Darling, My Hamburger* Bodley Head, Books for New Adults

ZINDEL, P. (1969) *The Pigman* Bodley Head, Books for New Adults; Armada Lion; Macmillan Education Topliner

5 Reluctant readers eleven to sixteen – policy and provision

John L. Foster

Headmaster, Lord Williams's Lower School East,
Thaine, formerly Head of the English Department,
Redefield School, Oxford

There is no doubt at all in our minds that one of the most important tasks facing the teacher of older juniors and younger secondary pupils is to increase the amount and range of voluntary reading. We believe that there is a strong association between this and reading attainment, and that private reading can make an important contribution to children's linguistic and experiential development.[1]

At a time when society is demanding a reassessment of classroom approaches and techniques in terms of how successful they are in promoting achievement in basic skills and in preparing young people for their economic roles in a technological society, it is important that the value of the time spent in encouraging voluntary reading should not be underestimated. The command of language demonstrated by those secondary pupils who read extensively in their leisure-time is often considerably greater than that of their contemporaries who do not read so widely. For, as the Schools Council's research team led by Frank Whitehead pointed out in their report on children's reading interests:

> there are good grounds (including some research evidence) for believing that, where it exists, this habit of wide independent reading has a massive influence for the good on the child's mastery of the written patterns of language; and we also suspect that it can have a far-reaching influence on the child's attitudes and values and on the whole picture he builds up of the world around him.[2]

Developing in pupils an interest in books as one of the chief sources of ideas and of information and, therefore, a passion for reading should be one of the main objectives of every teacher. It is, of course, one of the prime concerns of the English teacher, who should regard it as his responsibility to keep a record of the reading habits of all his pupils. Indeed, a record of the secondary pupil's reading habits, as a means of monitoring his development as a reader, is as important as the notes and comments on his written work that the teacher keeps in his mark book are as a means of monitoring a pupil's progress in his writing. In its simplest form this record can consist solely of a list of books that a pupil has read over a given period, with a note of any magazines, comics or newspapers that he reads regularly. A more detailed reading profile can include a checklist of reading skills, which will enable the teacher to identify particular weaknesses and to modify his teaching programme accordingly.

The need to keep a close check on secondary pupils' reading habits is shown only too clearly by the findings of the Schools Council's research team. Whereas at ten plus forty-nine per cent of the children questioned were committed readers, reading three or more books per month, only thirty-two per cent of those aged fourteen plus read books at a similar rate. Moreover, while at ten plus only thirteen per cent of the age group reported that they were non-book readers, no fewer than thirty-six per cent of the fourteen plus age group said that they did not read any books at all. Among the boys aged fourteen plus the percentage of non-book readers was as high as forty per cent.

The report highlighted the problem faced by the secondary school teacher concerned with encouraging voluntary independent reading. The older a pupil becomes the more reading has to compete with other activities for a share of the pupil's leisure-time. The research team found that although the fourteen plus non-book readers included some pupils who were weak or backward at reading, the majority of them were fluent enough to read books, but chose not to do so. Most of them could be classified as reluctant readers rather than non-readers. Significantly,

68

eighty per cent of the non-book readers reported that they did in fact read regularly, but their reading consisted solely of comics or magazines.

If we are to prevent younger secondary pupils from losing the habit of book-reading and to rekindle an interest in books among older pupils who have become reluctant readers, our first consideration must be to ensure that our class libraries and school libraries offer them a wide enough choice of reading. The danger is that in our enthusiasm to get pupils to read literature of quality we may be inclined to set our sights too high too quickly. While certain young reluctant readers may be lured from their comic-reading straight into the world of good modern children's literature by the books of such authors as Rosemary Sutcliff, Penelope Lively, Alan Garner and Leon Garfield, many others require the type of bridge provided by such books as Roger Collinson's *Butch and Bax* (Transworld, Carousel) or Reginald Maddock's *The Dragon in the Garden* (Macmillan Education, Topliner). As the Schools Council report suggested, many secondary school class libraries and school libraries:

need to include in their collections a certain amount of 'non-quality' narrative which will act as an inducement to reluctant readers ... there is need for a more generous interpretation of standards of quality in this area, and a recognition that the relevant evaluation will not be in adult terms but in terms of the current emotional and intellectual maturity of the children concerned.

Although there is some evidence among older secondary pupils, particularly among the boys, that there is an increasing preference for informational books, nevertheless the experience of many teachers is that narrative books are those most likely to capture the interest of the reluctant reader. Whitehead's survey, conducted in 1971, showed that more than three-quarters of all the books read by his sample were within the category of narrative, in which he included biography as well as fiction. The emphasis in the class library must be on narrative and on providing as broad a range of writing as funds will allow. As one witness to the Bullock Committee put it:

> What often seems to go unrecognized is the really massive and massively varied provision of books which is absolutely essential if the class library is genuinely to meet the needs of a secondary class of lively mixed ability.

Similarly, there are strong grounds for arguing that if we are really serious about encouraging the reading habit among all our pupils, then more of our library funds need to be diverted to the fiction and biography sections in order to make available as comprehensive a range of narrative writing as possible.

The importance of doing more than just paying lip-service to the ideal of a comprehensive provision of narrative cannot be overstressed. Too often in the past the school's English department, after having had to spend the bulk of its book allowance on providing the set books required for examinations, has found itself unable to afford more than a handful of books from series for the reluctant reader such as Topliners, Getaway and Knockouts. Class libraries in the middle forms in secondary schools have become stocked with multiple copies of books set in previous years' O-level examinations, rather than with titles chosen for their suitability to the pupils' needs and interests. Yet if our class libraries are to be effective in attracting reluctant as well as committed readers, then they need to be stocked systematically.

In the present economic circumstances it is becoming increasingly difficult for the head of the English department to make money available for the purchase of books for class libraries. For, as the cost of providing set texts increases, so the amount left over for use on class libraries is eroded. Surely it is time that the spending of a disproportionate amount of the book allowance on examination texts for a minority of pupils was challenged. Is it right that between fifty per cent and seventy-five per cent of an English department's book allowance should be swallowed up in the purchase of examination texts for fifth and sixth form pupils?

Perhaps the time is fast approaching when we must consider, in order to provide books equally for all our pupils, asking those who wish to sit literature examinations to purchase some of their set books themselves. An alternative is for us to arrange for schools in a particular locality to pool their resources and to share texts that they use as class readers with lower forms. Similarly, schools with copies of texts that they no longer require could be encouraged to sell them to local authority teachers' centres. In this way central banks of texts could be built up by teachers' centres, which could then loan them to schools as and when they were required. Such a system would make for a far more efficient use of resources than our current practice of each school buying its texts independently and then allowing them to gather dust on the stockroom shelves until such time as they reappear on the O- or A-level syllabus. Until such changes are introduced a strong case can be put forward for each secondary school, as part of its general book-buying policy, making available a separate allowance earmarked specifically for the purchase of books for class libraries.

In making provision for the reluctant reader in either the class library or the school library the person responsible for book selection must attempt to look at the books under consideration from the point of view of the young people to whom he hopes they will appeal. In recent years there has been a rapid expansion in the publishing of books aimed at the reluctant teenage reader and they vary enormously in quality. At one end of the spectrum there are books such as Ann Leete's *Second Chance for Love* (Aerial Books) and Michael Hardcastle's *The Big One* (Nelson, Getaway), both of which are direct, fast-moving narratives lacking subtlety either of plot or characterisation. At the other, there are books such as Gunnel Beckman's *Mia* (Longman, Knockouts) and Robert Lipsyte's *The Contender* (Macmillan Education, Topliner), which, like any good novels, offer the reader insights into character, motives and human behaviour. When making our selection we need to bear in mind that the abilities and interests of reluctant readers vary enormously and to beware of letting our literary judgement cloud our vision. It is important that our selection should include those books, whatever their quality, that the reluctant reader will choose to read, rather than consist only of those books which we consider to have literary merit. A list of some of the titles that I have found most popular with eleven- to sixteen-year-olds in an urban secondary school is included at the end of this article.

The argument put forward against a policy of allowing pupils to read whatever books they choose, irrespective of their quality, is that it is pandering to them and that instead of helping them to develop as readers it encourages them to be satisfied with what is second- or even third-rate. Obviously this is a danger and no one would deny that a number of those who, in school, become avid readers of books in the Checkers, Topliner and Getaway series, will as adults develop their reading tastes no further than, for example, the popular Mills and Boon romances, the westerns of J. T. Edson or the thrillers of Mickey Spillane. However, unless we are willing to start where the reluctant readers want to start, rather than where we would like them to start, there is no doubt that many of them will remain non-book readers. Besides, whereas the reading tastes of some of them do not develop, those of many others do. The more they read, the more discriminating they become. Often the teacher can play an important part in helping to refine and to develop the young reader's taste. By recommending a particular book at the appropriate moment he can broaden the scope of a pupil's reading and by his presentation of books in the classroom he can both introduce pupils to the world of adult literature and help them to develop the skills of reading with insight.

Books for the reluctant reader eleven to sixteen

The following list consists of those books which experience has shown to be those that are widely read by reluctant readers in an urban secondary school in a social priority area. At least one copy of each book is stocked in the school library and in the case of the most popular books such as *Mia*, *Sam amd Me*, *The Outsiders* and *Gangs and Victims* we stock two or more copies.

In addition to our school library we run a system of class libraries. The books are stored either in a number of boxes or on a movable trolley and are made available by the English teachers both during and after their lessons. The class libraries have been built up over a number of years and consist almost entirely of paperback books. Where possible multiple copies of these popular titles have been purchased. The class libraries are well used and we have to restock them annually. However, we regard encouraging the reading-habit as so central to our task that we consider it is essential to set aside part of our capitation allowance for this purpose.

Because the books are in constant use it is often difficult to keep track of them and no method that we have yet devised of checking them in and out has proved entirely satisfactory. Many teenagers, like many adults, keep a book at home long after they have finished reading it. Consequently, in order to cut down on losses, in the second half of the spring term each year we have an amnesty, which has become known as 'Bring-Back-A-Book Week'. The response is usually very good and on one occasion over 1,000 books were brought in during the week. We encourage the pupils to bring in any books from home that are no longer wanted there. In this way we supplement our class libraries with paperback books that they or their parents have bought and read, and no longer want.

The literary quality of the books in this list varies enormously, so it is necessary to stress that these titles make up only a part, rather than the whole, of our total class library stock. Alongside them on the trolley and in the boxes are included a wide range of Puffins and Penguins, as well as books from educational series such as the New Windmill series (Heinemann), the Athena series (Wheaton) and Imprint books (Longman). Nor is it an exhaustive list. Many of the authors of the books that I have listed have written other books, which have proved successful with the older reluctant reader.

In order to give some indication of the nature of the books in the list, I have placed them in a number of categories, according to the type of story that they tell. Obviously such a division is arbitrary and the categories overlap. However, I hope that this arrangement will help teachers and librarians with the task of book selection and to introduce teenagers who have enjoyed one particular book to another similar one.

Adolescence

Baker, Geoffrey *Sky High* Nelson, Getaway

The central character, Terry, a teenager, has just moved to a seaside town but does not think much of it and is similarly disenchanted with his new school. He becomes obsessed with a live wartime shell, which he finds on the beach, and moves into a den that he prepares for himself. An undemanding book from which readers can go on to the Topliners by Reginald Maddock and Christopher Leach.

Barstow, Stan *Joby* Heinemann Educational Books, New Windmill; Corgi

Set in the summer of 1939 when Joby is eleven. His mother has to go into hospital and while she is there Joby gets involved with Gus Wilson and his gang and the whole security of his home is threatened when his father runs off with his cousin Mona. An absorbing story, often enjoyed as a class reader. Possible follow-ups for fluent readers include Keith Waterhouse's *There is a Happy Land* (Longman, Imprint Books) for the boys and Winifred Cawley's *Gran At Coalgate* (Oxford University Press) for the girls. Slower readers can be offered Reginald Maddock's Topliners *Sell-Out* and *The Pit* (see below). The script of the television version of *Joby* is available in the Blackie Student Drama series.

Chambers, Aidan *Marle* Heinemann, Pyramid

The story of an adolescent boy who has been brought up on the island of Marle off the north-east coast, of his first love and of the pressures and conflicts he feels as he tries to decide whether to go to live and work in Newcastle or to stay on the island where his parents and grandparents have spent their lives.

Doubtfire, Dianne *Escape on Monday* Macmillan Education, Topliner

Popular, undemanding story about a teenage girl's conflicts with her mother about her clothes, going out and especially her new boyfriend, Terry. The particular reason behind her mother's harsh treatment of Veronica is revealed in a melodramatic climax. Other books which readers might be encouraged to try next include Geraldine Kaye's *Penny Black* (see below), Pamela Sykes' *East, West* (see page 102) or Dorothy Clewes' *Ginny's Boy* (see page 100).

Kaye, Geraldine *Marie Alone* Heinemann, Pyramid; Macmillan Education, Topliner

The story of a young typist who is about to leave home to share a flat with some friends from work when her parents' marriage collapses, and of how she copes with the situation and emerges from it more grown-up. The experiences of Karen, an American girl in similar circumstances, is told in Mary Blair Immel's *Two-Way Street* (Scholastic).

Kaye, Geraldine *Penny Black* Heinemann, Pyramid

Penny is sixteen, taking her O levels, but finding it difficult to concentrate on her work. Her mother is ambitious and possessive and there is constant friction between her and Penny over matters such as homework, staying out and taking a Saturday job in a supermarket. Torn between her mother, her own wish to leave, her boyfriend Mike and a new teacher at school on whom she gets a crush, Penny is eventually able to decide for herself what she wants to do with her life. A more demanding story about a girl about to leave school, trying to decide what to do, is told in Kenneth Wood's *Gulls* (Dobson) (see page 120).

Leach, Christopher *Answering Miss Roberts* Macmillan Education, Topliner

Seventeen-year-old Katie is in borstal, when she is asked to write an essay about herself. She tells of the shock she experienced when she discovered she was adopted, the resentment she felt when her foster-mother remarried and of how her search for her real mother ended in a clash with the police. The sequel, *Decision For Katie* (Macmillan Education, Topliner) describes how on leaving borstal she takes a job in the country, looking after a ten-year-old boy, in the hope of making a new start away from her unsympathetic home. But she finds that Graham and his parents are in the middle of a family crisis and she is forced into the position of having to take sides. Girls who enjoy these books about Katie can then be offered Barbara Boyers' *Search for Susan* (Dobson), another story about an adopted girl, her dreams of finding her real mother and how when she leaves school and takes a job a strange coincidence enables her to find out more about herself and to come to terms with reality.

Leach, Christopher *Tomorrow in Atlantis* Dent; Macmillan Education, Topliner

A novel about a frustrated fourteen-year-old London schoolboy Dave, who dreams of running away to California, and about what happens when he tips his schoolbooks into the canal and sets off in search of his own Atlantis. Two further stories about Dave are told in *A Temporary Open Air Life* (Dent; Macmillan, Topliner) (see page 118) and *Searching For Skylights* (Dent).

Maddock, Reginald *Sell-Out* Macmillan Education, Topliner

Danny Rowley is desperately upset when he discovers that his mother intends to remarry, for he had been very attached to his dead father. Suddenly he feels that everyone is against him and he is involved, as a result, in clashes with his family, a local gang and the police. A book full of incident, telling the story of Danny's problems within the framework of an adventure story about the criminal activities of the local gang and about Danny's school football team. Widely enjoyed by less experienced young secondary school readers.

Rosenberg, Sandra *Will There Never Be a Prince?* Macmillan Education, Topliner

The light-hearted story of Carol, an American teenager whose problem is that she is fat, her hang-ups about her weight and how she eventually finds a boyfriend by just being herself. Two similar stories are told in M. E. Kerr's very amusing *Dinky Hocker Shoots Smack* (Penguin, Puffin) in which Dinky eats to compensate for the fact that her parents spend so much time helping other people with problems that they neglect their own daughter, who is consequently driven to doing something drastic, and Maureen Stewart's *Orange Wendy* (Macmillan Education, Topliner), in which a clumsy, awkward, rather fat, Australian teenage girl falls in with a set of trendies and gets involved in shoplifting and drinking parties before she realizes their shallowness and goes on to form a relationship with another boy.

Adventure stories
Many pupils at the age of eleven have reading ages well below their chronological ages. Often the most appropriate books to offer these children are the shorter adventure-type stories to be found in series such as Club 75, Inner Ring Hipsters, Onward, Headlines, Rockets and Instant Reading, details of which are included in the annotated list of books for the backward reader in the secondary school on page 147. The transition from such books to longer ones needs careful handling and, as Olive Robinson suggests in her article, books must be found that cater

for the particular interests and needs of the individual student. This list mentions some of the books that have proved useful in helping younger secondary school pupils to make the required leap. A number of the books mentioned consist of short stories and can be introduced to the pupils by reading one or two of them aloud or, in the case of the Longman Knockouts series, by presenting them on the cassette tapes which the publishers produce.

The list may also prove useful with children who have become hooked on Enid Blyton's books. In many cases the spell proves extremely difficult to break and while reading Enid Blyton's books is preferable to reading no books at all, children will frequently continue to read them long past the stage at which they could have moved on to more demanding books, more appropriate to their age. The stories that I have found most successful in weaning pupils from Enid Blyton to other books are those in the Lone Pine series by Malcolm Saville. On other occasions books by E. W. Hildick, such as those about Lemon Kelly (Brockhampton) and Mabel Ester Allen's four books about the Wood Street gang (Methuen) have provided the necessary bridge. Once the pupil has come to realize that there are other authors, besides Enid Blyton, whose books he can enjoy, then he is often willing to move on to some of the adventure books mentioned below.

Andrew, Prudence *Ginger Over the Wall* Penguin, Puffin

An adventure story for younger readers about Ginger and his gang. Their secret hideout is discovered by a man who is on the run from the police. They have to decide whether to keep quiet and help him or to call the police.

Barry, Margaret Stuart *Tommy Mac* Penguin, Puffin

An entertaining book of short stories about the mischievous Tommy Mac, a ten-year-old, and the adventures that he gets involved in, such as being marooned in the snow with his lorry-driver father, when for a treat he goes with him on an overnight journey *Up the Great North*. Other stories describe Tommy's over-enthusiastic performance as a shepherd that ruins the form's Christmas play, how he falls off a fire-escape in a fight at school, and what he does to try to get rid of Aunt Lil when she comes to stay because Mam has the flu.

Collinson, Roger *A Boat and Bax* Transworld, Carousel

The story of how the summer holidays, which start uneventfully for Bobby Baxter, take an exciting turn when he and his friend Jugears find an old boat embedded in the mud beside the canal. They set about rebuilding her and what could have been a long, boring summer in Milbridge turns out to be one full of adventure, discovery and danger as Bax, Jugears and Worm sail off on a number of expeditions in *The Albatross*. What happens when Bax, out shopping for his mum at the market one day, sees some puppies at the pet stall and decides that he wants one, is told in *Butch and Bax* (Transworld, Carousel). Another book by Roger Collinson for younger readers is *Four Eyes* (Methuen). Set in a middle school it is the story of Ronnie Wicks, a bespectacled boy and a natural victim, and how he comes to terms with the leader of the bullies, Spud Murphy.

Dickenson, Christine *Dark Horse* Macmillan Education, Topliner

Tells the story of the opening of the Dark Horse Riding School at Lynham by young Yvonne Spencer and of her struggles against ill-fortune and hostility to get it established. An eventful horse story for younger girls, who can also be offered Michael Hardcastle's *The Chase* (Nelson, Getaway) and the many horse books by authors such as Ruby Ferguson, Christine Pullein-Thompson, Mary O'Hara, Marguerite Henry and Vian Smith.

Hildick, E. W. *Louie's Lot* Macmillan Education, Topliner

Tim Shaw, like all the other boys in his neighbourhood, wants to get into Louie's Lot, the group of boys who work the rounds for Louie, an unconventional milkman. Before he can join he faces all sorts of tests such as sorting the empties, reading the notes, the delivery race and the savage dog test. Even when he is in his adventures are not over, for there are other boys who want him out so that they can take his place. An entertaining, undemanding story for younger readers. Another adventure about Louie and his lot is told in *Louie's SOS* (Macmillan Education, Topliner).

Hildick, E. W. *Birdy Jones* Macmillan Education, Topliner

The first of four stories about Birdy Jones and his friend, Fixer Clarke, and the adventures that befall them in their attempts to make Birdy an international star as a pop whistler. As soon as they leave school they set off for London, where Fixer is sure that instant success will be waiting for them. The eventful story of their efforts to achieve fame is continued in *Birdy and the Group*, *Birdy Swings North* and *Birdy in Amsterdam*, all available in the Topliner series.

King, Clive *Me and My Million* Penguin, Kestrel

Ringo's brother Elvis plans to steal a picture worth a million pounds, but it all goes wrong when Ringo, who is not very good at reading and figures, gets on a number fourteen bus instead of a forty-one and ends up in a launderette in Putney instead of Tottenham Hale. With only ten pence in his pocket Ringo is forced to spend the night on an underground platform where he meets Angel Jim. From then on he is involved in a series of slapstick adventures, the final outcome of which is that everyone hails him as a hero rather than a villain. A very funny story that can be offered to those who have enjoyed the author's *Stig of the Dump* (Penguin, Puffin).

Layton, George *A Northern Childhood – The Balaclava Story and other stories* Longman, Knockouts

Five stories about a young boy growing up in a northern town.

Originally written for radio, they are very good for reading aloud. Three are available on cassette read by the author himself, including the extremely amusing title story, which is as popular as Bill Naughton's *Seventeen Oranges*. Another selection, *The Fib and other stories* is also available in the Knockouts series.

Leeson, Robert *The Third Class Genie* Collins, Armada Lion

The entertaining story of Alec, a working-class boy, who discovers a beer can that is sealed but obviously empty and from which there comes the sound of snoring. When Alec decides to investigate and opens the can out pops a genie called Abu. He puts himself at Alec's disposal and a series of amusing adventures follow.

Maddock, Reginald *The Dragon in the Garden* Macmillan Education, Topliner

One of the best-sellers in the Topliner series, with a wide appeal among the nine to thirteen age range. Tells the story of the dilemma that faces thirteen-year-old Jimmy when he moves to a new home, starts school for the first time in his life and immediately finds himself in conflict with the local bully, Fagso Brown.

Maddock, Reginald *The Pit* Macmillan Education, Topliner

Set in a small town on the edge of the moors in the north of England, *The Pit* tells the story of Butch Reece, a boy whose home background is such that if trouble occurs then it is Butch who is immediately suspected. But Butch is not a thief, although he knows who did commit the crime of which he is accused. The story of how Butch's true character is revealed to the people of his home town comes to a climax on the Pit, a deadly bog out on the moors.

McBratney, Sam *Mark Time* Abelard-Schuman

A week in the life of an eleven-year-old boy growing up in

Northern Ireland. It is the week when he learns that he has won a grammar-school place, but his concern is as much with the preparations for the 'battle' which is scheduled to take place between his gang, led by the Shampoo Kid and the gang 'across the line'. Although the action builds up somewhat slowly, it is nevertheless a book that many younger secondary pupils enjoy.

Naughton, Bill *The Goalkeeper's Revenge and other stories* Heinemann Educational Books, New Windmill; Penguin, Puffin

Thirteen stories about boys and the escapades that they get involved in. The title story happens to be about football, but it is not a collection of sports stories. The stories range from the hilarious *Seventeen Oranges*, in which a boy literally eats the incriminating evidence, to *Timothy*, the sad story of what happened to Mrs Peckerlea's budgie when she left it with Jimmy and his parents while she went on holiday. It also includes the much anthologized story of *Spit Nolan* and his trolley. The most popular short-story collection with the middle-school age range over the last decade.

Naughton, Bill *A Dog Called Nelson* Heinemann Educational Books, New Windmill

A lively, humorous first-person narrative, set in Bolton between the Wars, telling the story of the family that used to live 'in the bottom end house of our street'. It is the story of Noggy, eldest of six, of his stepfather Jud, a rag-and-bone man and pigeon fancier, of his mother Ranee, a 'terrific chopper of wood' and 'a cricketer too – a tremendous batter', and of their assorted animals, a donkey, a cat and the one-eyed mongrel dog, Nelson. Especially it is the story of Nelson – minding the younger children, dealing with the bailiffs, snoring through the silent pictures at the cinema and making an unrehearsed appearance in the top act at the variety theatre.

Pearce, Philippa *What the Neighbours Did* Penguin, Puffin

A collection of eight well-written short stories that are very popular with younger pupils. Includes *In the Middle of the Night*, the amusing story of an unforgettable midnight feast, *The Great Blackberry-Pick*, an account of a family blackberrying expedition that ends in a row and *Lucky Boy*, about a boy whose plan to spend an afternoon exploring on his own is ruined because he has to take his neighbour's young girl along with him.

Sudbery, Rodie *Rich and Famous and Bad* Transworld, Carousel

An amusing adventure story for younger girls telling what happens to Polly Devenish when she invents a boy-friend and to prove his existence writes a letter to him and, astonishingly, receives a reply. Another Polly Devenish story is told in *Warts and All* (Transworld, Carousel) in which Polly, now at technical college, decides to hold a party to celebrate getting a room of her own, but finds herself without the necessary money. She thinks up an unusual way of solving the problem, which produces unexpected results.

Taylor, Theodore *The Cay* Heinemann Educational Books, New Windmill; Penguin, Puffin

Widely enjoyed by small groups and classes of less fluent readers. Tells the story of a shipwrecked twelve-year-old white boy, temporarily blinded, and his companion, an elderly negro, against whom he is initially prejudiced. Other adventure stories popular with such groups include Armstrong Sperry's *The Boy Who Was Afraid* (Heinemann Educational Books, New Windmill) and *Old Mali and the Boy* (Heinemann Educational Books, New Windmill).

Townsend, John Rowe *Gumble's Yard* Penguin, Puffin

When their uncle and aunt disappear Kevin and Sandra make a secret home for themselves and their young cousins in what appears to be a deserted warehouse. It turns out to be used by a gang of crooks and the children find themselves besieged and then kidnapped before the mystery is solved and the criminals captured. Possible follow-ups include some of the books in the thrillers section, such as those by Alan Evans and David Line.

Contemporary

Adams, Philippa *A Hitch on the Way* Macmillan Education, Topliner

A hitch-hiking story for girls. Jan runs away from home, bound for London. She has several rather improbable adventures before she is eventually reunited with her family and everything works out all right in the end. An undemanding book, useful with the very uncommitted, inexperienced book-reader who is still relying heavily on comics and magazines for her reading.

Arundel, Honor *The Girl in the Opposite Bed* Macmillan Education, Topliner

Two girls from very different backgrounds and with very different personalities meet in hospital. Jane, who is having her appendix out, is shy and apprehensive and at first hates everything about the hospital. Jeanne, on the other hand, is cheeky and bouncy, at least on the surface. The story tells of how they react to one another and of the understanding that eventually develops between them. Other books by Honor Arundel include *A Family Failing* (Scholastic), which describes the emotional problems and tensions among the children of a one-parent family, *Emma in Love* (Pan, Piccolo) and *The Two Sisters* (Heinemann, Pyramid) (see page 99).

Baker, Geoffrey *Summertime Blues* Nelson, Getaway

The adventures of Peter and Stuart during a hitch-hiking holiday on the continent. Similarly straightforward narratives are available in the sequel, *Running Hot and Cold* (Nelson, Getaway), when the two boys take temporary jobs in a hotel, and in Jean Saunders' *The Fugitives* (Heinemann, Pyramid), see page 124.

Beckman, Gunnel *Mia* Bodley Head, Books for New Adults; Longman Knockouts

Translated from the Swedish by Joan Tate, *Mia* tells of one week in the life of a seventeen-year-old Swedish girl, who thinks she is pregnant. The reader shares Mia's anguish as she considers what she might have to do. Mia's problems are further complicated by the fact that her parents are in the process of separating.

Beckman, Gunnel *The Loneliness of Mia* Bodley Head, Books for New Adults; Longman Knockouts

The sequel to *Mia*, in which Mia is shown feeling lonely and confused now that her parents have separated and her relationship with her boy-friend Jan has come to an end. Mia becomes interested in the Women's Movement, meets another boy, Martin, and through the relationship which develops between her and her grandmother is helped to come to terms with herself and her new situation.

Beckman, Gunnel *Nineteen Is Too Young to Die* Macmillan Education, Topliner

First published in Great Britain as *Admission to The Feast*. Annika has learned that she is suffering from a fatal illness. The book takes the form of a letter to her closest friend in which she tries to sort out her confusion and distress by looking back over the events of her life and attempting to discover what it means. Fluent, older readers who find this book absorbing might be directed to Patricia Windsor's *The Summer Before* (Macmillan Education, Topliner Redstar). Its central character, Alexandra, has had a breakdown following the death of her closest friend, Bradley. The book is the story of how she learns to accept his death.

Brattstrom, Inger *Since That Party* Macmillan Education, Topliner

An unusual story about a group of Swedish teenagers, which centres around Nicholas, an awkward, clumsy unattractive boy, very much the outsider. It tells of his birthday party and the tragedy that follows it, showing how it affects the various members of the group. For older readers, who might then try Max Lundgren's *Summer Girl* (Macmillan Education, Topliner) (see page 101).

Breinburg, Petronella *Us Boys of Westcroft* Macmillan Education, Topliner

Not as compelling a read as the superb cover or dramatic blurb suggest, for the central story-line is not strong enough. Most successful with older, fluent readers, it tells the story of Walter Collins, a black boy living in a children's home in Kent, and his attempts to avoid getting mixed up in any trouble that occurs at his comprehensive school, because the threat of Borstal is hanging over him.

Browne, Tom *Me and Dicko and the DJ* Macmillan Education, Topliner

Appeals to boys who are interested in sound systems and mobile discos. Tells how the narrator and his friend Dicko, helped by friendly advice from a professional DJ, build their own disco and eventually perform at their first gigs.

Dhondy, Farrukh *East End at Your Feet* Macmillan Education, Topliner

Winner of the 1977 Other Award. Six well-written stories about the difficulties and challenges that face British and Asian teenagers living and growing up in the East End of London. The stories are told with humour and sympathy. Includes *KBW*, a moving story about a boy who is the victim of racial prejudice.

Similar books are difficult to find. Two possible follow-up books are Ray Pope's *Is It Always Like This?* (Macmillan Education, Topliner) (see page 94) and Rachel Scott's *A Wedding Man Is Nicer Than Cats, Miss* (Heinemann Educational Books, New Windmill), a teacher's account of teaching a junior class that included Hindus, Sikhs and Muslims as well as local Yorkshire children.

Dickenson, Christine *Siege at Robins Hill* Macmillan Education, Topliner

Janice is the eldest of five children whose parents have been killed in a fire. The book tells the story of her determined fight to keep them together despite the attempts of a number of adults, including awkward relatives, the Children's Department and the police, to split them up. The reader of Christine Dickenson's books can be encouraged to move on to other authors such as Honor Arundel, Geraldine Kaye, Christopher Leach and Jean Saunders.

Falk, Ann Mari *A Place of Her Own* Scholastic

Translated from the Swedish by Annabelle MacMillan. Tells the story of Stina, a fifteen-year-old who is orphaned and forced to move from the country to Stockholm to live with her older married sister and describes the difficulties she faces adjusting to her new life.

Heywood, Marion *Rose Red* Heinemann, Pyramid

Rose wants to do something to change the world and decides to start in Greenhill where she lives. She joins the local action group. Her mum thinks it is a waste of time, while her dad thinks she is just tinkering with the system. However, Rose is a determined character; but so too is Danny Malone. The book describes the relationship that develops between them as a result of Rose's involvement with the action group. A lively, often humorous story.

Hines, Barry *Kes* Wheaton, Athena; Penguin

First published as *A Kestrel for a Knave* and made into an award-winning film starring David Bradley. The story of Billy Casper, a boy from a broken home, bewildered by school life and uncertain what to do as the time to leave approaches, and of the kestrel that he finds and trains and that comes to mean so much to him, until he is robbed of it by his brother Jud, following a quarrel that Billy himself precipitates. Popular even when read as an examination text. Other books that can be offered as follow-up reading include Keith Waterhouse's *There Is a Happy Land* (Longman Imprint), short stories by writers such as Stan Barstow, Sid Chaplin, Bill Naughton and Alan Sillitoe, or plays such as Shelagh Delaney's *A Taste of Honey* (Methuen) and Keith Waterhouse and Willis Hall's *Billy Liar* (Blackie, Student Drama). An adaptation of *Kes* as a play, by Barry Hines and Allan Stronach is published by Heinemann.

Kamm, Josephine *Young Mother* Heinemann Educational Books, New Windmill

The story of a sixteen-year-old unmarried mother. A straightforward, undemanding narrative that is still widely read. Another book on the same theme is Honor Arundel's *The Longest Weekend* (Hamish Hamilton).

Mildiner, Leslie and House, Bill *The Gates* Centreprise

Written by two London teenagers, who themselves had similar experiences, it tells of two boys who stay away from school because they are school phobics. Describes what they do in order to avoid going to school, the special tutorial group that they attend and the school for maladjusted children to which they are eventually sent. Useful, because rather surprisingly there are few books about truants and how they spend their time, though its length makes it rather daunting for some reluctant readers.

Morpurgo, Michael *Long Way Home* Macmillan Education, Topliner

A boy who is fifteen and has already been in several foster homes goes to yet another one, this time on a farm with a family called the Dyers. The book tells of the ups and downs during the formation of the relationship between him and them and how, as a result of some emergencies that occur, they learn to accept one another. An undemanding story with a reasonable amount of excitement in it. Possible follow-ups are Catherine Cookson's *Mattie Doolan* (Pan, Piccolo) or Christine Dickenson's *Last Straw* (Macmillan Education, Topliner).

Rodman, Maia *Tuned Out* Macmillan Education, Topliner

Set in the summer of 1967, the story of two American brothers and of what happens when the younger one Jim discovers that Kev, who has just come back from starting college, is on drugs. Another American book on the same subject that is read with great interest by older teenagers is the anonymous *Go Ask Alice* (Corgi).

Zindel, Paul *The Pigman* Macmillan Education, Topliner; Collins, Armada Lion

John and Lorraine, two American teenagers, make a random phone call. The man who answers is a lonely widower, Mr Angelo Pignati, whom they come to know as the Pigman, because of his collection of china pigs. Taking it in turns they tell the story of the relationship that develops between them and of the tragedy that results from their youthful thoughtlessness and high spirits. Possible follow-ups for older fluent readers are William Corlett's *The Gate of Eden* (Bodley Head, Books for New Adults; Macmillan Education, Topliner Redstar) and Patricia Windsor's *The Summer Before* (Macmillan Education, Topliner Redstar).

Gangs and victims
Although the skinhead craze has passed, books like *Skinhead*

and *Boot Boys* remain very popular with certain reluctant readers. This list suggests a number of titles that we can offer as alternatives to such books.

Cormier, Robert *The Chocolate War* Gollancz

A compelling book that appeals to older boys who are fluent readers and who want books about the way things are, provided that they can be lured beyond the initial chapter in which they have to come to terms with the fact that the book is American and set in a New England Catholic boys' school. It is the story of how an evil teacher enlists the aid of a school gang to help him to sell 20,000 boxes of cheap chocolates at a vast profit in order to further his own ambition to become Headmaster, and of how one student, Jerry Renault, refuses to be intimidated. Possible follow-ups are Glendon Swarthout's *Bless the Beasts and Children* (Heinemann Educational Books, New Windmill; Macmillan Education, Topliner Redstar) about a group of misfits in an American summer camp and the desperate mission they undertake to free a herd of buffalo who are to be shot for the amusement of tourists – a book which is both a savage attack on some American values and an authentic account of the conflicts of adolescence – or J. D. Salinger's *The Catcher in the Rye* (Penguin).

Daniel, Susie and McGuire, Pete (eds) *The Painthouse* Penguin

In their own words an East End skinhead gang talk about how the gang was formed, what they used to do together and what membership of the gang meant to them. They give their own views on authority, violence, the gang, the police and schools. For older fluent readers.

Foster, John L. (ed) *Gangs and Victims* Nelson, Getaway

The best-seller in the Getaway series. Several of the stories are violent, but in each case the suffering of the victim is clearly brought out. The most popular stories appear to be Evan

Hunter's *The Last Spin*, the tragic story of a friendship that develops between two boys from rival gangs as they settle a dispute by playing Russian roulette, and Michael Hoyland's *The Slug* about a boy who is so terrified of the local bully that he won't even tell his parents what's wrong after the bully has fired an airgun slug into his back. Readers who have enjoyed *The Last Spin* can be offered Evan Hunter's *Blackboard Jungle* (Four Square) and then E. R. Braithwaite's *To Sir, with Love* (Heinemann Educational Books, New Windmill; Four Square).

Green, Janet *The Six* Bodley Head, Books for New Adults; Longman Knockouts

Written by a Bristol schoolteacher in conjunction with one of her classes, this consists of six separate stories by the members of a skinhead gang. The style is very colloquial and there is a considerable amount of violence. But there is humour as well, particularly in Joe's story in which the gang ambush another gang as they are breaking into a tobacconist's. And the authors themselves put the actions of the six into perspective with one of their final comments, 'We weren't really a skinhead gang, just a bunch of kids playing at the games that happened to be the thing at the time'. Those who enjoy this book can then be given *The Painthouse* (see above) to find out what real skinheads thought and did.

Hinton, S. E. *The Outsiders* Collins, Armada Lion

Written by Susan Hinton at the age of seventeen, *The Outsiders* tells of gang rivalry in an American city between the Greasers, from the poorer East Side, and the Socs, the West-Side rich kids. It is an action-packed story with threats, a murder in self-defence, a flight from the police, a dramatic fire rescue, a rumble and finally two deaths. The events are described through the eyes of Ponyboy, one of the Greasers, whose two friends die. A book that both boys and girls enjoy.

Hinton, S. E. *That Was Then, This Is Now* Collins, Armada Lion

The story of how two boys, Bryon and Mark, who have always been like brothers, gradually, at the age of sixteen, drift apart, and of how as they do Bryon finds that all the old answers no longer satisfy him. During the year of the story a barman friend of theirs is killed in a brawl, Bryon meets a girl whose friendship becomes more important to him than Mark's, he is beaten up for a trick that Mark played, and his girlfriend's younger brother gets mixed up in the drugs scene. Finally, when Bryon discovers that Mark is a pusher, he is faced with the decision of whether or not he should inform the police. Like *The Outsiders* a very popular book.

Hinton, S. E. *Rumblefish* Longman, Knockouts

The central character of *Rumblefish* is Rusty-James, a fourteen-year-old boy, who idolises his elder brother, the Motorcycle Boy, once the leader of the Packers. Rusty has been in the reformatory for five years. Looking back he tells the story of the time after his mother disappeared, when he was living with his alcoholic father, acting tough, fighting and drinking, trying to gain for himself the reputation that The Motorcycle Boy had had. The narrative moves quickly and dramatically from one event to the next until he tells of the night when his dream is finally shattered.

Jamieson, Alan *The Carnferry Gang* Edward Arnold

Designed for older pupils with reading difficulties, this consists of fifteen stories about a group of five children who live in an industrial town in Scotland. Their various adventures lead them into conflict with each other as well as with authority. Stories such as *Fighting Talk, The Break-In, The Janitor's Day Out*.

McGrath, Pat *The Green Leaves of Nottingham* Hutchinson, Unicorn

Written in five weeks while the author was in between schools in London at the age of fourteen, this novel gives a teenager's view of slum-street life. The central character is a young boy who returns to Nottingham in his early teens after a spell in Borstal, only to get further involved in crime. The obvious follow-up books are Alan Sillitoe's *The Loneliness of the Long Distance Runner* (Pan). *A Sillitoe Selection* (Longman Imprint) and *Down to the Bone* (Wheaton), Brendan Behan's *Borstal Boy* (Corgi) and the short stories of Bill Naughton, Sid Chaplin and Stan Barstow.

Paice, Margaret *Run to the Mountain* Collins, Armada Lion

A tough and exciting book telling the story of three boys who are on the run from a Sydney boys' home – Jacko, hard and ruthless, who planned the break-out, Beetles, who agreed to go with him, and Eddie, who had no choice when he stumbled on the others as they were about to leave and was forced to go along when Jacko held a piece of broken glass to his throat. At first things go well and Beetles and Eddie do as Jacko says, until he robs a petrol station and is killed in a car crash. Scared though they are, Beetles and Eddie struggle on until Beetles too is involved in an accident and Eddie is forced to give himself up in order to fetch help. A fast-moving story that appeals to readers of S. E. Hinton's books.

Pointon, Barry *Cave* Bodley Head, Books for New Adults

Ian Thompson is about to leave school and is looking forward to a trip to Belgium as a passenger in his dad's lorry before starting work with the same transport firm as employs his father. But when his mother is called away because his brother, who is serving in Northern Ireland, has been shot, Ian finds himself left at home alone to look after his young sister, Karen. There is trouble brewing though between Ian and Cave, a local gang leader to whom Ian has sold a worn-out motor-cycle cylinder for three pounds. The story moves to an exciting climax at a fair and Ian's fight with Cave leads to an unusual ending. The simple, direct narrative makes it a suitable book for the inexperienced older reader.

Pope, Ray *Is It Always Like This?* Macmillan Education, Topliner

The story of Pinky's gang, who have their headquarters in the blocked-off arch of a railway viaduct in south-east London. One day they find two young children there, a boy and a girl, who say their parents have gone away and that they are terrified of being sent to a home. The gang try to cope themselves, but have to draft in a girl to help. At first the girl, Pat, feels lonely and insecure, doesn't get on with the gang and insults one of them, Tormon, a British Pakistani. Gradually, however, she learns that the gang need her and could like her, and that Tormon, whose strangeness frightened her, is kind and understanding and that he is lonely too. Other stories about children trying to cope with problems on their own are Christine Dickenson's *Siege at Robins Hill* (Macmillan Education, Topliner) (see page 87) and Jill Paton Walsh's *Fireweed* (Macmillan; Penguin, Puffin), see page 127.

Sherry, Sylvia *A Pair of Jesus Boots* Heinemann Educational Books, New Windmill; Penguin, Puffin

Serialized on television as *Rocky O'Rourke*, this story was written while the author was living in Liverpool, and is set in its back streets. It deals with teenage gangs, break-ins and an unstable family, one of whom is in prison after being framed. An American reviewer described it on its publication in 1969 as:

> a superior specimen of the new realism in children's literature. It's an adventure story in which the motivation is not the wish for adventure but the driving force of poverty and hunger, a story of companions in what ought to be misery but is not.

Other stories about big city life that younger secondary readers might go on to enjoy are Paula Fox's *How Many Miles to Babylon?* (Penguin, Puffin), about a small boy captured by a gang of bigger boys, who terrorize him into kidnapping dogs and hiding them under a derelict fun-fair, while they wait for the owners to bring a reward, Emily Neville's *It's Like This Cat* (Penguin, Puffin), a year in the life of a fourteen-year-old New York boy, or Rodie Sudbery's *A Curious Place* (André Deutsch), the story of Philip Gray and what happens when his family move to Glasgow and he meets up with Gordon and his gang.

Wilson, Roy *One Long Sunday* Heinemann, Pyramid

A fast-moving story about a group of boys who run away from a remand home. Within twenty-four hours they are back in custody, but not before one of them has received a badly cut arm and a shotgun has been fired. The tensions that develop between the boys, as they argue about where to go and what to do, make this an exciting read. Other books that deal with boys on the run from homes are Roy Brown's *Flight of Sparrows* (Abelard-Schuman) and Margaret Paice's *Run to the Mountain* (Collins, Armada Lion) (see page 93).

Ghosts, horror and the supernatural

Stories about ghosts, horror and the supernatural are popular with young readers throughout the eleven to sixteen age range. One particular problem, as far as the reluctant reader is concerned, is to ensure that he chooses books that are not beyond his capability. Paperbacks with lurid covers, such as *Ghosts* (Macmillan Education, Topliner), which contains some rather demanding Victorian stories, may catch the reluctant reader's eye and cause him to pick up a book which is not suitable for him because it is too difficult. This list gives details of some less demanding books, from which readers can then move on to the innumerable collections of ghost and horror stories published for older teenagers and adults.

Carew, Jan *Save the Last Dance for Me* Longman, Knockouts

Four stories of the supernatural, simply written, presented in large print, and short enough to be accessible to those with a limited concentration span. Includes *The House*, about a man whose uncle leaves him a house which casts a spell over him and changes his whole life, and *Save the Last Dance for Me*, about a girl whose boy-friend died in a motor-cycle accident after they had quarrelled and who had promised to kill her if ever she danced the last dance with anyone but him.

Chambers, Aidan *Haunted Houses* Pan, Piccolo

Immensely popular. Eleven stories of supposedly real hauntings. Also in the Piccolo True Adventure series are the same author's *More Haunted Houses*, *Great British Ghosts* and *Great Ghosts of the World*, and published by Kestrel *Aidan Chambers' Book of Ghosts and Hauntings*.

Chambers, Aidan *Ghosts 2* Macmillan Education, Topliner

Nine ghost stories, seven by Aidan Chambers and two by Brian Morse. A good range of stories including hauntings on a honeymoon and in an undertaker's, as well as the very amusing *Dead Trouble*, about a ghost having problems with his hauntings because his death occurred when he fell into a concrete-mixer and his remains have ended up encased in a concrete pillar fifty feet above the ground, so that although he has disappeared no one knows for certain that he is dead.

Danby, Mary (ed) *The Ninth Armada Ghost Book* Collins, Armada

The most recent of the very popular Armada Ghost Books. Other similar collections include *Spooky Stories* (Transworld, Carousel) edited by Barbara Ireson, *Ghosts, Spooks and Spectres* edited by Charles Molin (Penguin, Puffin) and *Ghostly Gallery* (Penguin, Puffin), chosen by Alfred Hitchcock.

Groves, Paul and Grimshaw, Nigel *Thirteen Ghosts* Edward Arnold

A book of specially written ghost stories suitable for the slower reluctant reader who finds the most popular collections too difficult. The situations in some of them are clichéd, but the first one, about Uncle Ben's leg, which thumps round the house after its owner's death, is very amusing. Because it is designed as a schoolbook, rather than just a reader, it contains questions on the stories.

Holroyd, Sam *Ghosts 3* Macmillan Education, Topliner

Thirteen stories specially written for the Topliner series and offering a much easier read than Aidan Chambers' selection *Ghosts* (Macmillan Education, Topliner), in which many of the stories are inaccessible to the inexperienced reader because of the complexity of their vocabulary and style.

Hurwood, Bernhardt J. *Vampires, Werewolves and Other Demons* Tandem, Target

Stories of strange beasts and supernatural beings. Younger fluent readers can go on to Lucy Berman's *The Creepy-Crawly Book* (Tandem, Target) or the author's companion volume *Ghosts, Ghouls and Other Horrors* (Tandem, Target). Older readers can be offered Jim Alderson's adaptation of Bram Stoker's *Dracula* (Hutchinson, Bulls-Eye).

Jackson, Anita *Spirals* Hutchinson/ILEA

Six books of simply written supernatural stories with strong story-lines, short enough to be read and enjoyed by those with limited reading stamina. *The Actor* describes how the career of the great Alex Bolt began when he played the part of a ghost, or rather when a ghost played it for him. *The Ear* is a grisly tale about a painter who thinks he is Van Gogh. *Bennet Manor* tells of a mysterious man from the past who saves a young girl from

97

being murdered by her uncle, while *The Austin Seven* is the story of a man who buys a haunted car and breaks his back in a crash which leaves the vehicle undamaged. *Dreams* tells of how a young station porter foresees and then witnesses a terrible train crash, and *A Game of Life and Death* is about a man who buys an unusual chess set which enables him not only to defeat, but to kill his opponent – provided he wins!

Pepper, Dennis (ed) *Ends and Escapes* Nelson, Getaway

Short stories by Roald Dahl, Ray Bradbury, Frank Sargeson and others. Similar collections are available in *In Fear and Dread* (Nelson, Getaway), edited by Arthur J. Arkley, *Mystery and Suspense Stories* (Ward Lock Educational, WLE Short Stories), edited by John L. Foster, and Kathleen Lines's two collections *The House of the Nightmare* (Heinemann Educational Books, New Windmill) and *The Haunted and the Haunters* (Heinemann Educational Books, New Windmill).

Sherburne, Zoa *The Girl Who Knew Tomorrow* Scholastic

Angie Schofield is different from other girls because she has the gift of extra-sensory perception. As a result she becomes a nationwide television star, recognised everywhere she goes. At first she enjoys her fame, but later longs to be just like any ordinary teenager. A book with a wide appeal because it deals with the glamorous world of show business as well as with the fascinating subject of ESP. Two other novels by Zoa Sherburne available in this country are *Jennifer* (Scholastic), the story of a girl who lives in daily fear that her mother, an alcoholic, will have a relapse, and *Stranger in the House* (Scholastic) about Kathy, whose mother returns home after nine years in a mental hospital.

Tate, Joan *You Can't Explain Everything* Longman, Knockouts

Two short, simply written stories which will be widely enjoyed. In *The Wooden Man* a boy finds in a junk shop a strange wooden figure which enables him to see into the future. At first he is excited at having such powers and keeps them a secret, until he himself falls ill and, after consulting the figure, becomes convinced that he is going to die. *The Bubbles* is the story of a remarkable day in the life of teenager Teresa, who suddenly finds that she can read the thoughts of the people she meets when they start appearing in bubbles over the people's heads. Other books that readers of these stories might enjoy are those by Jan Carew and Anita Jackson.

Love stories
Arundel, Honor *Emma in Love* Pan, Piccolo

Emma is sixteen, living in Edinburgh, going to school there and at the same time keeping house for her student brother Richard. Tells the story of her life in Edinburgh and the development of her relationship with Alastair, a Glasgow University student. Another book by Honor Arundel often enjoyed by reluctant readers is *The Two Sisters* (Heinemann, Pyramid), the story of Geoff and Maura, a young couple in love and wanting to marry, although they have practically no money, and of the problems they have to face.

Banks, Lynne Reid *My Darling Villain* Bodley Head, Books for New Adults

A first-rate novel for teenagers, the story of the relationship that develops between typically middle-class Kate Dunhill and sixth-former Mark Collins, from a working-class family, following Kate's first small mixed party, which gets out of hand when a mob of gatecrashers arrives. Possible follow-ups include other novels in the Books for New Adults series by Paul Zindel, Peggy Woodford and William Corlett and adult novels such as the author's *The L-Shaped Room* (Longman Imprint Books), Margaret Drabble's *The Millstone* (Longman Imprint Books) and the novels of Edna O'Brian.

Cleary, Beverley *Fifteen* Penguin, Puffin

The story of the summer when Jane Purdy, a fifteen-year-old American girl, meets and dates her first boy-friend. A book that continues to be very popular.

Clewes, Dorothy *Ginny's Boy* Heinemann, Pyramid

The story of Ginny, who has always wanted to be a nurse, but isn't sure if she will get good enough exam results, and her relationship with good-looking Don, who says that he is a motor-mechanic and takes her for trips on the back of a powerful motor bike. Ginny's conflicting emotions about what to do with her life, as she becomes more and more involved with Don, are finally resolved when he is forced into telling her the truth about himself and she is left enough money to pay for a crash course to obtain the qualifications necessary for a nursing career. Many girl readers also enjoy Dorothy Clewes's *A Girl Like Cathy* (Scholastic), about a girl coming to terms with her real identity following the death of her adoptive mother.

Daly, Maureen *Sixteen and other stories* Scholastic

Nine stories that deal with problems of teenage relationships, including *The Love Letters*, *Tall Grass* and *I Remember You*. Although they are about American teenagers the stories have a wide appeal, as does the author's *Seventeenth Summer* (Scholastic), the prize-winning story of a young American girl's first romance.

Foster, John L. (ed) *That's Love* Macmillan Education, Topliner

A popular collection of short love stories by authors such as Morley Callaghan, Joan O'Donovan, Bill Naughton and Walter Macken and including Evan Hunter's *On the Sidewalk Bleeding*. Two other collections edited by John L. Foster, *In Love, Out of Love* and *All for Love*, both containing stories specially written for the series by authors such as Sylvia Sherry, Rony Robinson,

Geraldine Kaye and Victoria Williams, are also available in Topliners.

Foster, John L. (ed) *First Love* Heinemann, Pyramid

Short love stories by Susan Price, Patricia Windsor, Christine Dickenson and others. A more demanding selection with stories by authors such as John Wain, Ernest Hemingway, J. B. Priestley and Stephen Leacock is available in the editor's *Love Stories* (Ward Lock Educational, WLE Short Stories).

Hewitt, Jenny *Judy in Love* Macmillan Education, Topliner

The story of how sixteen-year-old Judy falls in love for the first time and of the complications that arise because of her parents' opposition to the relationship. A similar story about Lisa and her relationship with Jim, whom her parents consider undesirable, is told in Dianne Doubtfire's *This Jim* (Heinemann, Pyramid).

Lundgren, Max *Summer Girl* Macmillan Education, Topliner

Translated from the Swedish by Joan Tate, the story of how a difficult, independent city girl is sent to spend the summer in the country with a family of strangers and meets a boy who is as independent-minded as she is. They form an uninhibited relationship and accidentally become involved in the enquiries into a strange and violent crime. For older readers, who can then go on to the author's *For the Love of Lisa* (Macmillan Education, Topliner Redstar), about a young married couple considering splitting up.

Martin, Vicky *September Song* Macmillan Education, Topliner

First serialized in *Honey*, the story of one September when, during the family's usual summer holiday, April falls in love with her cousin Paul. An undemanding book, which is useful because it provides a magazine-type story in book format and can be used to overcome the reluctance of those teenagers who will read magazines but reject books.

Oppenheimer, Joan L. *On the Outside, Looking In* Scholastic

An undemanding story about the relationship that develops between Laurie Kent, an insecure orphan, alone and frightened after the experience of a series of foster homes, and Bruce Larson, an emotionally crippled boy recovering from a leg amputation.

Robinson, Rony *Six Summers* Nelson, Getaway

An unusual, well-written love story describing the relationship stretching over a period of ten years between Alison, a girl from a wealthy Derbyshire family, and Tom, from a working-class one. The time is the 1930s and the relationship develops against a background of social and political change. The story is related from Alison's point of view. For the older reluctant reader who is ready to move on from the less demanding love stories and who, after reading *Six Summers*, might be offered Lynne Reid Banks' *My Darling Villain* (Bodley Head, Books for New Adults) (see above), Peggy Woodford's *Please Don't Go* (Bodley Head, Books for New Adults) or Ivan Turgenev's *First Love* (Penguin, Peacock).

Sykes, Pamela *East, West* Heinemann, Pyramid

The story of Julie, a typist whose parents are always quarrelling and who daydreams of marrying Dave and leaving home. When Dave returns from a long holiday abroad and her parents announce that they intend to get divorced Julie's romantic view of marriage is destroyed. Another book in which a girl is forced to come to terms with the fact that she cannot live in a dream world is Molly Cone's *The Real Dream* (Scholastic), the story of two American teenagers Lu and Hogie.

Sykes, Pamela *Early One Morning* Heinemann, Pyramid

A first-person narrative in which the author describes the thoughts and emotions of Vicki, a teenage girl who becomes involved with an older man.

Tate, Joan *Sam and Me* Macmillan Education, Topliner

One of the best-sellers in the Topliner series. The story of Jo, how she meets and falls in love with Sam but becomes so unhappy after their marriage that she takes someone else's baby. Other books by Joan Tate that can be offered as further reading are the two stories about Nibs and Clee, *Whizz Kid* (Macmillan Education, Topliner) and *Clipper* (Macmillan Education, Topliner), and *The Tree* (Heinemann, Pyramid), the story of the relationship that develops between Tina and David, a boy who is extremely shy and withdrawn.

Townsend, John Rowe *Goodnight, Prof. Love* Oxford University Press; Penguin, Peacock

The story of the relationship that develops between seventeen-year-old Graham Hollis, from a respectable middle-class home, and Lynn, a blonde, rather vulgar, waitress, while his parents are away on a short holiday, and of what happens when they elope. A romantic adventure story that, for all its improbability, has a wide appeal. A more convincing story of a relationship that develops between two teenagers from very different social backgrounds is told in Lynne Reid Banks' *My Darling Villain* (Bodley Head, Books for New Adults). Older fluent readers, who have read *Goodnight, Prof. Love*, can be offered John Rowe Townsend's other novel about teenagers' first experience of love, *The Summer People* (Oxford University Press), the story of two people who meet in the summer of 1939.

Walker, Mona Cotton *For The Love of Mike* Heinemann, Pyramid

An undemanding story about Mike, an artistic drop-out, and

Jan, a girl who becomes involved with him despite the fact that their outlooks on life are very different.

Zindel, Paul *My Darling, My Hamburger* Bodley Head Books for New Adults; Corgi

Extremely popular, a well-written novel, at times very funny, at others very moving, telling the story of American teenagers, Sean and Liz and Dennis and Maggie. In their final year at high school they double-date, cut classes, worry about their looks and about sex and how to handle it. A frank book about a group of ordinary teenagers learning how to cope with life and love. Paul Zindel is a writer with a remarkable flair for communicating with teenagers. His first novel *The Pigman* (Macmillan Education, Topliner; Collins, Armada Lion) is widely read and older, fluent readers appreciate the humour and insights of his two other novels for young people, *I Never Loved Your Mind* (Bodley Head, Books for New Adults; Collins, Armada Lion) and *Pardon Me You're Stepping on My Eyeball* (Bodley Head, Books for New Adults).

Science fiction

Science fiction stories, like supernatural stories, have a wide appeal throughout the eleven to sixteen age range. Fluent, committed readers move easily and naturally via books by authors such as Nicholas Fisk, John Christopher and Robert Heinlein to the adult science fiction stories of Arthur C. Clarke, Isaac Asimov, Ray Bradbury and J. G. Ballard. Others, who are capable but somewhat reluctant readers, start with the books based on television programmes – Tandem Target's *Dr Who* series, Star Books' *Bionic Man* and *Bionic Woman* series, Corgi's *Star Trek* books and Futura's *Space 1999* series – and then, with careful coaxing, can be persuaded to move on to more demanding short stories and novels. Many reluctant readers, however, find the books based on the television series rather difficult, for the writers of these novels make few concessions and the young reader needs both stamina and ability if he is to cope satisfactorily with them. The following list gives details of some science fiction books which are not too demanding and which can be offered to the young reader who is unwilling or unable to tackle more complex stories.

Carew, Jan *Stranger Than Tomorrow* Longman, Knockouts

Three short stories combining strong narratives with a simple sentence structure, particularly suitable, therefore, for the slower reluctant reader. *Greenfingers* describes the frightening results when an experimental fertilizer is fed to plants in an attempt to increase food supplies to combat the Great World Shortage; *The Soundmaker* tells of the stifling of individuality in the New State where the slogan is 'Reality is the only good'; and *'This planet is hostile . . .'* is a story in which the reader's expectations are reversed for the alien turns out to be man. Possible follow-ups are the science fiction stories of W. C. H. Chalk and Lee Harding (see below) or supernatural stories such as Anita Jackson's *Spirals* (see page 97) and the author's own *Save the Last Dance for Me* (see page 96).

Chambers, Aidan and Nancy (eds) *World Zero Minus* Macmillan Education, Topliner

Short stories of the future by writers such as Ray Bradbury, John Christopher, Isaac Asimov and Arthur C. Clarke. Quite a demanding selection, most suitable for older more fluent readers. Similar collections are available in *In Time To Come*, edited by Aidan and Nancy Chambers (Macmillan Education, Topliner) and *Science Fiction Stories* edited by John L. Foster (Ward Lock Educational, WLE Short Stories).

Chalk, W. C. H. *The Gnomids* Heinemann Educational Books, Booster Books

Probably the most popular of the easier science fiction stories, *The Gnomids* tells the story of the strange monkey-like creatures from under the sea, whose appearance on the surface of the earth threatens man's survival. Readers who enjoy it can be offered the two other science fiction stories in the Booster series, *Mask of Dust* and *The Man from Mars*, or abridged versions of John Wyndham's novels, such as *The Triffids*, adapted by Patrick Nobes (Hutchinson, Bulls-Eye), *The Chrysalids* adapted by Sue Gee (Hutchinson, Bulls-Eye) and *The Midwich Cuckoos* edited by Josie Levine (Longman, Knockouts).

Chalk, W. C. H. *The Conquest of Mars* Heinemann Educational Books, Instant Reading

A simply written, thought-provoking story about a group of earthmen who arrive on a planet intent on exploiting its natural resources and find themselves opposed by a community which is functioning happily without money, greed or violence. Other science fiction stories for young readers set on Mars include Lee Harding's *The Frozen Sky* (see below), James Blish's *Welcome to Mars* (Faber) and Hugh Walters' *Murder on Mars* (Faber).

Chalk, W. C. H. *The Terrible Things* Heinemann Educational Books, Instant Reading

The terrible things are giant, six-legged, flame-throwing towers which have dropped mysteriously one night from some flying machines. The narrator is a boy who has escaped death and with other survivors is trying to build a new life. A simply written story with a fast moving plot, which has a sequel *The Firebirds* (Heinemann, Instant Reading), set in the Isle of Wight. For younger readers.

Chilton, Irma *Take Away the Flowers* Heinemann, Pyramid

Two stories about a space transporter pilot, Tom Davies, working for the United World Government. In *Take Away the Flowers* a strange weed is choking the crops and causing famine on Ultima, the most distant planet. Tom is sent out with a cargo of weedkiller, but is mysteriously diverted to a planet inhabited by beautiful blue flowers with telepathic powers. The story tells of his struggle to break free from the hold they begin to exert over his mind. In *Fuller's World* Tom visits a private planet to negotiate with its owner, Fuller, a recluse, on behalf of the UWG who want to use the planet as an intermediate space station. Tom becomes a prisoner of Fuller's staff of obedient robots before he discovers the truth about Fuller's planet. Possible follow-ups are John Kirkhain's *The Beasts of Plenty*, Irma Chilton's *String of Time* (Macmillan Education, Topliner) and *Spray of Leaves* (Macmillan Education, Rockets).

Clarke, Arthur C. *Islands in the Sky* Penguin, Puffin

A space-mad boy, Roy Malcolm, wins a television contest and is sent on a visit to the Inner Station, a space centre circling 500 miles above the Earth, where spaceships are refuelled and repaired. Other stories for younger fluent but reluctant readers about boys involved in space adventures include John Christopher's *The Lotus Caves* (Penguin, Puffin), in which two boys living on the moon go exploring and crash through its surface into an eerie and fantastic world, and Raymond F. Jones's *Moonbase One* (Abelard-Schuman).

Harding, Lee *The Frozen Sky* Cassell, Patchwork Paperbacks

The colonists on Mars are threatened by a strange sickness. The spaceship from Earth bringing the medical supplies that can save them crashes in a remote part of the planet. *The Frozen Sky* tells the story of how the crew of the giant land-crawler Goliath attempt to salvage the cargo. Also by Lee Harding, *The Fallen Spaceman* (Cassell, Patchwork Paperbacks), about a small being from outer space encased in a huge spacesuit, who falls from his reconnoitering starship and is found by two boys, one of whom becomes trapped inside the giant suit.

Harrison, Harry *Spaceship Medic* Penguin, Puffin

The exciting story of a young doctor on his first voyage who suddenly finds himself responsible for a badly damaged spaceship and its panic-stricken crew after a collision with a meteorite. Possible follow-ups are Nicholas Fisk's *Space Hostages* (Penguin, Puffin), in which a group of children investigating a spaceship are kidnapped and find they have to fly the machine themselves, and Alan E. Nourse's *Rx for Tomorrow* (Faber), a collection of tales of science fiction, fantasy and medicine.

Nation, Terry *Rebecca's World* Beaver

An amusing and highly imaginative fantasy story for younger readers. Rebecca is mysteriously transported to a distant planet through her father's astral telescope. It is a strange world where everyone lives in fear of the GHOSTS. In the company of Captain K, Grisby and Kovak, three unusual individuals who befriend her, Rebecca sets off into the Forbidden Lands in search of the last Ghost Tree, the wood of which can be used to dissolve the GHOSTS. *En route* there are riddles to be solved, strange beings like the Swardlewardles and the Tongue-Twister Monster to be outwitted and an ever-present threat from the greedy Mister Glister, who, aided by his henchmen Lurk and Cringer, wants the tree all for himself. A book from which readers might be encouraged to go on to the books of C. S. Lewis, Alan Garner and Ursula Le Guin.

Pepper, Dennis (ed) *Through Time and Space* Nelson, Getaway

Seven stories by authors such as Ray Bradbury and Alan E. Nourse and including Arthur Porges's *The Ruum* and Arthur C. Clarke's *Before Eden*. Also in the Getaway series *Far Out*, edited by Arthur J. Arkley, with stories by Frederick Pohl, Damon Knight and others.

Walters, Hugh *Blast Off At Woomera* Faber

The first of a series of space adventure stories about Chris Godfrey and his friends. While still a schoolboy Chris is involved in a dangerous space experiment. Other books about Chris and his 'astrotec' friends, published by Faber, include *First Contact? Passage to Pluto* and *Tony Hale, Space Detective*.

Williams, Victoria (ed) *Future Love* Macmillan Education, Topliner

Seven stories of love in the future. A fairly demanding selection including Ray Bradbury's amusing tale of the last man and woman alive on Mars, *December 2005 – The Silent Towns*, Michael Delving's *The Girl with the Humming Heart*, about a robot just built for loving, and Jack Finney's *The Other Wife*, about a man who lives in two worlds at the same time and has a wife in each! For older, fluent readers who might then go on to Louise Lawrence's *Andra* (Macmillan Education, Topliner Redstar) or Jane Yolen's selection *Zoo 2000* (Macmillan Education, Topliner Redstar).

Young, Peter *Once Upon a Space* Schofield and Sims, Data

Three stories for pupils with a reading age of eleven to twelve years. *Look-See on Planet Rokh* and *The Dead Planet* are space exploration stories. *Day of the Doom* describes an undersea civilization in which the lives of the inhabitants are strictly controlled and from which Iso and Milo decide to escape rather than live as slaves, and to discover for themselves whether the Doom above the sea is really as dangerous as the Teller has told them it is.

Sport
In spite of the large part that sport often plays in their lives, the number of fictional sports books for reluctant readers is relatively small. One reason for this is that it is difficult to write convincing

sports fiction. All too often the events described in a football story, for example, appear either ridiculous and contrived, or trivial and insignificant, when compared with the real-life drama of last Saturday's match, television highlights, newspaper reports and articles in magazines like *Shoot*. Brian Glanville's stories are a notable exception. Another reason is that few people have yet created fantasy figures comparable to those whose exploits were recounted week by week in the popular comics of the 1940s and 1950s – *The Wizard, The Hotspur, The Rover* and *The Champion* – heroes like Limp-Along Leslie, the international inside-forward with a limp, Nick 'It's Goals That Count' Smith, Ishmael, the gypsy centre-forward, and the incredible Wilson, the first three-minute miler, the man whose bouncers went for six byes and shattered the sightscreen behind the wicket-keeper's head! One writer who has created such a figure is Robin Chambers, whose first book, *The Ice Warrior and other stories* (Penguin, Kestrel), includes a story about Oduwole, star of Zaire's 1994 World Cup Team, a footballing wizard whose banana kick bends the ball through incredible angles.

The following list includes books about boxing, motor-racing and running, as well as about football.

Bateman, Robert *Young Footballer* Pan, Piccolo

A football story for younger readers about a boy whose second season with the Woodside Comets is threatened, for it seems that his team will be out of the County League before the end of the year. Other authors of similar stories are Michael Hardcastle and Sean McCann (see below).

Carter, Bruce *The Bike Racers* Longman, Knockouts

Traces the road-racing career of Jim Newton as he progresses from tinkering with an old motor bike, via sidecar-racing, to racing a borrowed 750cc solo bike. There is plenty of mechanical detail for the teenage motor-cycle enthusiast to enjoy and the Knockout edition includes a simplified diagram of parts of a bike and of two racing circuits. A possible follow-up is Michel-Aimé Baudouy's *Mick and the Motorbike*, about how Mick spends his holiday restoring a discarded bike, which he then wants to race, even though he is under age.

Cate, Dick *On The Run* Macmillan Education, Topliner

Three short stories about running. *Going to the Dogs* is about a boy and his grandad who go to an illegal greyhound race and have to make a run for it when the local policeman arrives. *Cock o' the North* is the story of Chris, good at running at school, and how he suddenly decides to take it up again a few years after leaving and becomes good enough to go in for the Dale Run, the race that decides who is the North's best cross-country runner. *A Split Second*, set in the 1930s, is about running for money on the makeshift tracks of the Durham coalfields, where the races are fixed and unscrupulous managers issue the orders, place the bets and share out the winnings. An obvious follow-up is Sid Chaplin's *The Leaping Lad and Other Stories* (Longman, Imprint).

Chambers, Aidan *Cycle Smash* Heinemann, Pyramid

Pete is a promising athlete who is involved in a motor-cycle accident. The book tells the story of how he comes to terms with the consequences of his injury.

Cope, Kenneth *Striker* (BBC)

Based on the BBC series *Striker*, the book tells the story of Ben, Bomber, Soggy and the other members of the Brenton boys' football team, both on and off the field, on their way to winning the cup. For younger readers.

Foster, John L. *Sports Stories* Ward Lock, WLE Short Stories

Twelve short stories covering eight different sports. Authors include Brian Glanville, Joan Tate and Gerald Sinstadt. Three of the stories are very amusing: Samuel Selvon's *The Cricket Match*, about a West Indian boy inspired by the West Indies' success in a test series against England who boasts of a prowess that he does not possess; Michael Parkinson's *Clakker May*, the story of a very eccentric goalkeeper; and Alun Richards's *Hon. Sec.* (RFC), in which the Hon. Sec. saves Pontlast RFC's Easter tour from ending in a disastrous scandal.

Glanville, Brian *Goalkeepers Are Crazy* Longman, Imprint Books

A collection of twelve sports stories, nine of them about football, many of them presented as first-person narratives. The driving force of the central characters is their passionate interest or involvement in sport and the stories show the effects on their lives of their dedication, ambitions, fanaticism and obsessions. Readers who enjoy this collection will probably enjoy Brian Glanville's other collection *A Bad Lot and Other Stories* (Penguin, Peacock) and his novels, *The Olympian* (Pan), the story of a talented runner and his eccentric coach, who is determined to make him a champion, and *The Rise of Gerry Logan* (Hodder and Stoughton), a footballing novel about a brilliant inside-forward.

Glanville, Brian *Goalkeepers Are Different* Penguin, Puffin

The best football novel to have been written for young people, it charts the career of teenage goalkeeper Ronnie Blake, from his trial with Borough, through his apprenticeship and on to his first Wembley appearance. What makes this an outstanding book is the authenticity of its detail, which so many other football novels for children lack. Possible follow-ups are Eamon Dunphy's *Only a Game* (Penguin, Peacock), an account of what a professional football career is like for the ordinary player, Barry Hines's first novel *The Blinder* (Penguin, Peacock), the story of Lennie Hawk, a larger-than-life teenager and brilliant footballer and his exploits both on and off the field, or David Storey's *This Sporting Life* (Penguin).

Hardcastle, Michael *Goals in the Air* Heinemann, Pyramid; Pan, Piccolo

The story of a sixteen-year-old footballer, Kenny Rider, and how he gets his chance with his local club, second division Marton Rangers. His successes on the field are offset by difficulties at home, with his father who wants him to find himself a proper job, and with his girl-friend Sandra. He loses his place through injury, regains it, then at the end of the story breaks his leg. An easy read for those who like football fiction, but lacking the authentic background detail which makes Brian Glanville's football writing outstanding. Kenny Rider's attempts to re-establish himself following his broken leg are told in a sequel, *Where the Action Is* (Heinemann, Pyramid). Michael Hardcastle has also written a series of books about a young footballer, Mark Fox, published by Armada, four books about football at school-boy level – *United, In the Net, Free Kick* and *Away From Home* (Methuen) – and *Heading for Goal* (Nelson, Getaway).

Lipsyte, Robert *The Contender* Macmillan Education, Topliner

Set in New York, the story of Alfred Brooks, a seventeen-year-old from Harlem, who sets out to become a boxer, and of how he learns to contend with the harsh world of the ghetto. Readers who find *The Contender* absorbing often also enjoy Martin Ballard's *Dockie* (Collins, Armada Lion), about a London docker's son in the 1920s who take up boxing, see page 117.

McCann, Sean *Goals For Glory* Brockhampton

An adventure story for younger readers about the fortunes of the Drove's End boys football team, which is enjoyed by those who like Kenneth Cope's *Striker* and Michael Hardcastle's undemanding football stories. The team's further adventures are recounted in the sequel *We Are The Champions* (Brockhampton).

Rutherford, Douglas *The Gunshot Grand Prix* Collins, Armada Lion

One of a number of books, such as *Killer on the Track* (Collins) and *Race against the Sun* (Collins), in the Chequered Flag series about a young racing driver, Tim Ryder. In *The Gunshot Grand Prix* he finds himself dragged into the plottings of an underground terrorist group. A similar story is told in *Road Race* by Philip Harkins (Scholastic) and Bruce Carter describes the heartbreaks and triumphs of a young grand prix driver, Nick, in *Four Wheel Drift* (Heinemann, Pyramid). Two other books about motor-sport are Bruce Carter's story about the Le Mans twenty-four-hour race, *Speed Six* (Penguin, Puffin) and Pierre Cestex's *The Nightmare Rally* (Tandem).

Terson, Peter *Zigger Zagger* Penguin

Avidly read, Peter Terson's play tells the story of a school-leaver, Harry Philton, his school and family background, his search for the right job and his Saturday afternoons at the City End with Zigger and the other fans. Finally Harry is shown making the choice between the excitement of Zigger's way of life and a safe steady job, but the question of whether he couldn't be an apprentice *and* a football fan remains.

Westwood, P. S. *Rider of the Night* Oliver and Boyd

The first of three books in a speedway series, specially written for reluctant readers. Together with the other two books, *Wheels of Fortune* and *Junie*, it makes up a full-length novel describing the hero's experiences of leaving school, finding a job, entering the world of speedway, falling in love and getting married. Very much a formula book and the presentation is off-putting with work exercises included and an unfortunate title, Read, Write and Enjoy. However, there are few speedway stories for reluctant readers, apart from autobiographies, and young speedway fans often enjoy the series.

Wilson, Roy *First Season* Macmillan Education, Topliner

Together with its sequel, *Season in Europe*, it tells the story of Danny Martin's first season as a professional footballer with first division Lundchester City. Both books have rather contrived crime stories as sub-plots, but are popular with football enthusiasts.

Non-fiction sports books
Many teenage sports enthusiasts prefer non-fiction books. This list gives details of some that have proved popular.

Croall, Jonathan *Don't Shoot the Goalkeeper* Oxford University Press, Standpoints

An examination of all aspects of football and the part it plays in our lives, in a lively magazine format.

Dunphy, Eamon *Only a Game* Penguin, Peacock

An account of what a football league career is like for most professional footballers.

Edmundson, Joseph *Great Moments in Boxing* Transworld, Carousel

Mainly about heavyweights with accounts of some of the epic bare-fist fights as well as Patterson v Johansson and Ali v Frazier.

Emery, David *Lillian* Blackie, Kennett Library

An abridged version of David Emery's story of the career and tragic early death of his fiancée, Olympic athlete Lillian Board.

Foster, John L. *Athletics Champions* Nelson, Interest

Stories of the achievements of nine great Olympic athletes including Abebe Bikila, Paavo Nurmi, Jesse Owens and Al Oerter.

Foster, John L. *Football Champions* Nelson, Interest

Accounts of how the eleven British clubs who have won European competitions in the past decade achieved their successes.

Glanville, Brian *The Puffin Book of Football* Penguin, Puffin

A clear account of the history of football, including the growth of tactics and the development of the game throughout the world, as well as in England.

Goodbody, John *The Topliner Book of Football* Macmillan Education, Topliner

Information on all aspects of football and including a section of advice on how to improve one's own game.

Hooper, Royston *Moto-Cross* Macmillan Education, Topliner

A handbook for scrambling enthusiasts, who also enjoy John Dyson's *The Motorcycling Book* (Penguin, Peacock).

Pierce, Roger *The Puffin Book of Freshwater Fishing* Penguin, Puffin

An introduction to freshwater fishing for the beginner, describing the tackle required, the different types of fish, where they are to be found, and moving on to accounts of the thrills of fly-fishing, spinning and advanced 'fieldcraft'.

Tagholm, John *Football: How much do you really know?* ITV, Look-In Books

Fascinating details on aspects of football not often written about. Sections, for example, on the pitch, players' kit, floodlights, referees and linesmen, and the contents of a trainer's bag.

Starting out
Stories of teenagers who are about to leave school and are

looking for a job, or about those who have just left and their first experiences of work and of adult life, appeal to older readers. An increasing number of such books are now available and it is interesting to reflect how different in style and content these books are to the career novels of the 1950s (see Sheila Ray's article pages 47–8).

Andrew, Prudence *Goodbye to the Rat* Heinemann, Pyramid

A realistic story about three working-class boys in a large industrial town who are about to leave school, describing their search for jobs. The TV script *Terry* by Alan Plater in *Scene Scripts* (Longman, Imprint Books) edited by Michael Marland, about a boy who has tried a number of jobs but can't find any that he likes, is a possible follow-up.

Ballard, Martin *Dockie* Collins, Armada Lion

Set in London's dockland in the 1920s, the story of a boy who leaves school to follow in his father's footsteps and become a docker. Times are hard, work is scarce and there's trouble between the union and the port bosses. Moggy Harris and his father Curly have conflicting views about the union's action. Meanwhile Moggy is taking his first steps as a professional boxer in the hope of escaping from the world of poverty and uncertain employment in which the dockers live. A book that the urban teenager of the 1970s finds readily accessible.

Clewes, Dorothy *Nothing to Declare* Heinemann, Pyramid

Dave is unemployed, having left school and been unable to find the job he wants as either a mechanic or a driver. When a stranger offers him a job driving vans from Newhaven to Dieppe, then back across the channel and on to London he accepts only too readily. As a result he becomes involved in smuggling over illegal immigrants and, after a narrow escape, finds out as a result of the experience what job he really wants to do. Michael Hardcastle tells a similar, but less demanding story in *Money for Sale* (Heinemann Educational, Guided Readers).

Kamm, Josephine *The Starting Point* Heinemann Educational Books, New Windmill

Deals convincingly with some of the problems that can face a young married couple, such as living with in-laws while searching for a place of their own. Simply written it provides an absorbing read for unbookish teenage girls. A similar story is told in Honor Arundel's *The Two Sisters* (Heinemann, Pyramid).

Leach, Christopher *A Temporary Open Air Life* Dent; Macmillan Education, Topliner

The sequel to *Tomorrow in Atlantis* (see page 76). Dave has decided not to stay on at school to get more qualifications, but is uncertain what to do. He takes a job as a labourer while he tries to make up his mind. Working life turns out to be very different from school life and by the end of the story he has plenty of ideas about what he wants his own life to be like and what he is determined to avoid. A book for older, less skilled readers, who are in their final years of schooling, who can then be offered Christopher Leach's third book about Dave, *Searching for Skylights* (Dent).

Lingard, Joan *Into Exile* Heinemann Educational Books, New Windmill; Penguin, Puffin.

The third book in Joan Lingard's series of stories about two Belfast teenagers Sadie, a Protestant, and Kevin, a Catholic. They are married and living in London. Shows clearly the difficulties that a young couple may encounter starting their married life in a small flat in a big city. Teenagers who enjoy it can be offered the two earlier books about Sadie and Kevin, *The Twelfth Day of July* (Penguin, Puffin) and *Across the Barricades* (Penguin, Puffin), and the sequel *A Proper Place*

(Hamish Hamilton), which shows them continuing their search for a place to live where no one will mind the differences in their religion and in which they can bring up their newly-born son.

MacGibbon, Jean *Jobs for the Girls* Heinemann, Pyramid

The story of two London girls who find themselves stranded in Devon with nowhere to stay and no money, and who manage to obtain holiday jobs. There is excitement and romance, and as a result of their experiences the girls realize what they want for themselves in the future. Jean Macgibbon's other book in the Pyramid series is an obvious follow-up. Also set in Devon, *After the Raft Race* tells the story of Patty, a London girl whose father is in prison and whose mother is living under an assumed name, and of how she is afraid to make friends until Terry asks her to crew his craft in the Totnes Raft Race.

Parker, Richard *Quarter Boy* Heinemann, Pyramid

An amusing and light-hearted story about a boy who has just left school and finds a job that he can really enjoy as a result of undertaking to repaint the Quarter Boy, a 400-year-old figure that is part of the town's clock. A book that appeals to readers who have enjoyed Christopher Leach's two Topliners *Tomorrow in Atlantis* and *A Temporary Open Air Life*.

Price, Susan *Sticks and Stones* Faber

A very readable story about Graeme who is sixteen and working in a supermarket. He is bored stiff and would like to become a park gardener, but he knows his dad won't be in favour of the change. To escape from the supermarket he is forced, therefore, to adopt a desperate plan. The account of Graeme's struggle to break away from his parents' domination and make his own choice of career and of the working life in a supermarket, which many teenagers have experienced, make this a book which has a wide appeal.

Saunders, Jean *Only Yesterday* Heinemann, Pyramid

Cathy is a school-leaver. She and her three friends, Alec, Val and Fergy are on the dole. One by one the others find jobs until Cathy is left feeling very much the odd one out. She finds herself clashing with her parents too, until one day her mum collapses and is rushed into hospital. A sympathetically told story of the uncertainty Cathy feels as she tries to find a satisfying career for herself.

Storr, Catherine *Who's Bill?* Macmillan Education, Topliner

A novel based on the ITV schools programme *Starting Out*, a ten part serial story aimed at older, less motivated, under-achieving students and designed to help adolescents to understand and to cope with some of the challenges that face them as they prepare to take their place in the adult world.

Tate, Joan *Ginger Mick* Heinemann, Pyramid; Longman, Knockouts

Ginger Mick is Liverpool Irish with flaming red hair and a temper to match it. He has no certificates, but is good with engines and when he gets offered a job in a Coventry motor works, he leaves home. A story about a boy adjusting to life at work, living in digs away from home, building a relationship with a girl and beginning to understand himself. Although there is not much detail about Ginger's motor bike or his work as a mechanic, the fact that he is interested in engines means that some boys who don't read much apart from motor-cycle magazines are willing to try it.

Wood, Kenneth *Gulls* Dobson

An account of three teenage girls growing up in a bleak, un-attractive town in the North-East, their last days at school and their first love affairs and experiments with sex. A sensitive, realistic novel for the older fluent reader.

Thrillers

Thrillers by authors such as Desmond Bagley and Len Deighton appear regularly on adult best-seller lists (see page 14). A number of older teenagers read such books, but, as with adult science fiction novels, many reluctant readers find their length daunting and, because many of them read slowly, lack the necessary stamina to sustain interest long enough to read them. This list includes details of some shorter thrillers, most of which have been specially written for young and inexperienced readers. In addition to these books, the Hutchinson Bulls-Eye series offers a number of shortened versions of popular adult thrillers, adapted to make them accessible to the older, less fluent reluctant reader. There are versions, for example, of several of the James Bond books and of Desmond Bagley's *Running Blind*, John Creasey's *Murder, London-New York* and Victor Canning's *The Scorpio Letters*. Similarly, the Aerial series, published by Cedric Chivers, includes retellings of John Midgley's *Donovan* and John Creasey's *Murder at Night*.

Bebbington, Roy *Diamonds High* Nelson, Getaway

A straightforward adventure thriller in which private investigator Van der Molen and his assistant Anje undertake to uncover the Diamond Trail – a smuggling organization that stretches from Amsterdam to Kentucky. Their efforts involve them in an exciting chase across Canada and the USA.

Borisoff, Norman *You Might Even Like It* Scholastic

A tense, well-structured story about Debbie and her boyfriend Kenny, who impulsively attacks a pusher selling drugs to a young teenager and finds himself caught up in a network of intrigue involving police corruption as well as drug-pushing. A fast-moving adventure for older readers.

Buchanan, Peter *The Marco File* Longman, Knockouts

Six stories about Marco, a hired assassin, whose assignments take him all over the world – Italy, Africa, England and Spain – and frequently to Switzerland to visit his friend, the ingenious gunmaker Pierre Stoeller. In the final story, *Bullet For Sale*, Marco himself is outwitted and killed. A controversial book, which teenage addicts of television crime programmes take in their stride, but which can be criticized as being as amoral as certain adult thrillers.

Evans, Alan *Running Scared* Brockhampton; Beaver

A short, gripping story of three children, Neil, Sheila and Squib Lang, and how they come to the aid of Brent, a secret service man on the run from a gang of villains in bleak hill country. Somehow one of them must get to a telephone to pass on a vital message from Brent, who has an injured ankle. The tension is skilfully maintained and there is an exciting chase at the climax. A second adventure involving Squib is told in *Kidnap!* (Brockhampton). On holiday with a school party in France he is mistaken for the son of a rich French businessman and finds himself and three other children being hunted by a gang of kidnappers. Readers who enjoy these books can be offered Richard Parker's *Snatched* (Penguin, Puffin), another kidnapping story, set against a background of contemporary political events.

Hardcastle, Michael *On the Run* Nelson, Getaway

One of several undemanding and rather implausible stories of crime and adventure by Michael Hardcastle. In *On the Run* three young people on a package holiday in Malta get involved in some amateur detective work. The mystery ends in a chase through the Maltese catacombs. Michael Hardcastle's other thrillers include *Don't Tell Me What To Do* (Heinemann, Pyramid), about Tom who runs away from home and gets involved with a gang of drug-pushers, *Flare Up* (Nelson, Getaway), a mystery story set in the Welsh countryside, and *Get Lost* (Nelson, Getaway), about a hotel receptionist in a small seaside town who gets mixed up with two rival gangs.

Household, Geoffrey *Escape into Daylight* Heinemann Educational Books, New Windmill

An adventure and suspense story describing how Mike and Carrie, who have been kidnapped, make a desperate attempt to escape from their captors. For older, fluent readers, who can then be offered the author's *Rogue Male* (Heinemann Educational Books, New Windmill), about a spy in hiding after an assassination attempt, and *A Rough Shoot* (Heinemann Educational Books, New Windmill), about the unexpected events that ensue when a retired colonel takes a pot shot at someone whom he thinks is a poacher, or Victor Canning's two adventure stories about a boy called Smiler, *The Runaways* (Heinemann, New Windmill) and *Flight of the Grey Goose* (Heinemann, New Windmill). There is also a simplified version of *The Runaways*, suitable for less fluent reluctant readers, in the Heinemann Guided Readers series.

King, Adam *Who Wants To Be a Dead Hero?* Macmillan Education, Topliner

A fast-moving mystery story in which David Brand, seeking to find out exactly how his father died in what seemed at first to be an accident, becomes involved in an international assassination plot and finds his own life in danger. Other Topliner thrillers include Joan Aiken's *Nightfall*, about a young painter, Meg, who has a haunting dream about her past which leads her into a mysterious murder in a Cornish village, and Stuart Jackman's *The Golden Orphans*, in which journalist Val Murray investigates the mysterious appearance in a remote corner of New Zealand of three young Chinese who have apparently been washed ashore.

Line, David *Run For Your Life* Penguin, Puffin; Heinemann, New Windmill

Serialized on television as *Soldier and Me*, a well-written suspense story involving two children who overhear a murder plot which no one will believe and find themselves being chased by a ruthless gang. Its successor, *Mike and Me* (Heinemann Educational Books, New Windmill; Penguin Puffin), the story of Jim Woolcott, his cousin Mike, their eccentric art teacher Moggy, and a gang of vicious thugs who want to destroy their town in order to make a fortune, was described by one reviewer as a 'refreshing cliff-hanger thriller'.

Prowse, Philip *The Woman Who Disappeared* Heinemann Educational Books, Guided Readers

Designed for foreign learners of English and written, therefore, with a careful control of vocabulary and structure, this book provides the slower reluctant reader with a fast-moving thriller. Private eye Lenny Samuel is employed to find a missing girl and in the course of the assignment he is hit on the head, nearly killed and chased by the police, before solving the mystery. Other easy-to-read thrillers in the Heinemann, Guided Readers series include Philip Prowse's *Bristol Murder*, Michael Hardcastle's *Money For Sale* and Piers Plowright's *The Smuggler*.

Saunders, Jean *Nightmare* Heinemann, Pyramid

A suspense story in which two teenagers, Rick and Jenny, locked overnight by mistake in a department store, are held to ransom by two desperate crooks. Those who enjoy it can be encouraged to read the author's *The Fugitives* (Heinemann, Pyramid), the story of how Pete, a teenager on a hitch-hiking holiday meets a young runaway girl and decides to help her to return to her foster parents in Cornwall, and of how they dodge the police and parry the curious questions of the people they meet.

Treece, Henry *Ask For King Billy* Faber

An adventure story for younger readers about Gordon Stewart, a private detective whose agency seems to be a complete failure. He is on the point of giving up when he is given a mysterious assignment, which leads to an eventful journey in search of the solution. Those who enjoy it can be offered Henry Treece's other thriller *Don't Expect Any Mercy* (Faber).

Walden, Amelia *Where Was Everyone When Sabina Screamed?* Scholastic

An unusual adventure story set in Morocco, featuring a girl detective, Lisa Clark, and an assortment of colourful but sinister characters including a blond folksinger, who mysteriously disappears then reappears, the son of a Berber chief, a friendly guide who only wants to help, a beautiful night club singer, and a streetwise orphan who lives on his wits in the crowded bazaars of Marrakesh. An exciting suspense story for older, fluent readers.

War stories
A considerable number of stories with a wartime setting, both fictional and autobiographical, have been published recently, providing teenagers with insights into what life was like during the Second World War. Peggy Woodford's *Backwater War* (Bodley Head, Books for New Adults) and Esther Hautzig's *The Endless Steppe* (Heinemann Educational Books, New Windmill; Penguin, Peacock) are two examples. Such books, however, are often too demanding for the inexperienced reader. This list contains details of a number of novels and collections of true stories about the War that have proved popular with a wide readership. Other books that reluctant readers might go on to read are the detailed accounts of wartime experiences given in such books as C. E. Lucas Phillips' *The Cockleshell Heroes* (Pan), P. R. Reid's *The Colditz Story* (Hodder and Stoughton) and Paul Brickhill's *The Dambusters* (Pan), or the simplified versions of several of them that are available in the Kennett Modern Library series (Blackie) and the Bulls-Eye series (Hutchinson).

Chalk, W. C. H. *The Spider Bomb* Heinemann Educational Books, Booster

The story of an undercover British secret service agent, James Catchpole, working in Germany during the War and of the narrow escapes he has while locating the source of the deadly spider-bomb that is causing considerable damage to the British navy. Possible follow-ups are Richie Weaver's *True Spy Stories of World War Two* (Transworld, Carousel) or Ivan Southall's *Seventeen Seconds* (Brockhampton), an account of the work of bomb-disposal officers during the Second World War.

Chambers, Aidan *Fighters in the Sky* Macmillan Education, Topliner

First-hand accounts of their experiences by second world war pilots, giving a clear picture of the lives of fighter and bomber crews. A collection of extracts which can be used simply as a book of short stories or to stimulate the reader to go on to the books from which the passages are taken. For those very interested in flying follow-ups include *Aidan Chambers' Book of Flyers and Flying* (Penguin, Kestrel), Jan Mark's novel, *Thunder and Lightnings* (Penguin, Kestrel), about two boys, one of whom, Victor, is passionately interested in aeroplanes, Graeme Cook's *Wings of Glory* (Tandem, Target), true adventure stories of airmen during World War Two or, in the case of the older fluent reader, H. E. Bates's *Fair Stood the Wind for France* (Longman, Imprint Books).

Cook, Graeme *Commandos In Action* Tandem, Target

True stories of the commandos, their training and some of the dangerous missions they undertook during the Second World War. Two companion volumes by the same author, *None But The Valiant*, about the war at sea, and *Wings of Glory*, about the war in the air, are also available in the Tandem Target series.

Hoare, Bob *Great Escapes of World War II* Transworld, Carousel

A collection of true escape stories, which includes Colditz, The Great Escape and The Wooden Horse, as well as the story of the only German prisoner to escape from England. A book to give to those who would find the full-length escape stories too demanding and from which they might then go on to the simplified Kennett Library version of P. R. Reid's *The Colditz Story* (Blackie).

March, William *Company K* Nelson, Getaway

An abridged version of a book consisting of a collection of thoughts and incidents told by a group of American soldiers who were in the same company during the First World War. It accurately reflects what life was like in the trenches on the battlefields of northern France. The simplification has been skilfully done and the book loses none of its impact for being abridged. Older fluent readers might then go on to Erich Maria Remarque's *All Quiet on the Western Front* (Heinemann Educational Books, New Windmill).

Serraillier, Ian *The Silver Sword* Heinemann Educational Books, New Windmill; Penguin, Puffin

Serialized on television and translated into many languages, the story of four children as they make their way across Europe after the War in search of their parents. An immensely popular novel, full of incident, showing how the children grow up as a result of the experiences they have to face.

Walsh, Jill Paton *Fireweed* Macmillan; Penguin, Puffin

Suitable for group as well as individual reading, the poignant story of Bill and Julie, two teenagers hiding from the authorities in London during the blitz. Depending on their age and fluency, readers might then be offered Nina Bawden's *Carrie's War*

(Penguin, Puffin), or Sylvia Sherry's *Dark River, Dark Mountain* (Heinemann Educational, New Windmill).

Walsh, Jill Paton *The Dolphin Crossing* Macmillan; Penguin, Puffin

A story about two boys who took a boat and went to help the stranded British soldiers at Dunkirk. Possible follow-ups include Paul Gallico's *The Snow Goose* (Penguin) and Philip Turner's *Dunkirk Summer* (Hamish Hamilton).

Weaver, Richie *True Spy Stories Of World War II* Transworld, Carousel

A collection of true stories about some of the famous and infamous spies of the last war. The book also gives information about the different secret service networks and suggests other books that teenagers might like to read.

Westall, Robert *The Machine Gunners* Macmillan; Penguin, Puffin

Winner of the 1975 Carnegie Medal. A compelling novel, set in Tyneside during the early 1940s, combining authentic detail with skilful characterization, lively dialogue and an absorbing plot. A group of youngsters, Chas McGill and his friends, find a crashed German fighter plane with its machine gun undamaged. They dismantle it, hide it, and secretly set it up ready to wage their own war against the Germans, while the authorities hunt desperately for the missing weapon.

Westerns
Stories about the American West fascinate many younger secondary school children, as the popularity of television westerns illustrates. There are, however, relatively few simply written western adventures or collections of short stories about the West that have been specifically designed to appeal to the reluctant

reader. This list mentions some of the few such books available. Older readers can be offered the paperback westerns that are popular with adults. A useful list of some of the better examples of the genre, suitable for such pupils, can be found in the 'further reading' section in C. E. J. Smith's *Ten Western Stories* (Longman, Imprint Books).

Benedict, Rex *Last Stand At Goodbye Gulch* Heinemann Educational Books, New Windmill

Absurd and amusing, the story of fifteen-year-old Luke and his unlikely adventures among the badmen. A more straightforward western adventure is told in the author's *Good Luck Arizona Man* (Penguin, Puffin). For more fluent readers.

Chalk, W. C. H. *Jim Silent* Heinemann Educational Books, Instant Reading

Simply written, the story of the friendship that develops between Henry Page, a white settler, and an Apache Indian, Jim Silent, and of how it survives although they find themselves on opposing sides in the battle for the land around the township of Riverbend between the settlers and the US Cavalry and Geronimo and his Apaches. A book to offer to those who have enjoyed Albert Rowe's *Lone Wolf* (Macmillan Education, Club 75) or *Pollen Girl* (Macmillan Education, Rockets).

Chambers, Aidan *Snake River* Macmillan Education, Rockets

The story of how eighteen-year-old Clint tracks down two outlaws who have brutally attacked his father, and of the shoot-out at Snake River when he finally catches up with them.

Hirst, William *Stage to Nowhere* Nelson, Getaway

An undemanding adventure story about Sam Spencer and how he is at first suspected of robbing a stage, then later teams up with a Wells Fargo agent and helps to track down the bandits responsible. Two other simple westerns by the same author, also in the Getaway series, are *The Train Robbers* and *Lucky Mountain*.

Foster, John L. (ed) *Westward in their Wagons* Macmillan Education, Topliner

Nine short stories about pioneers and life in their homesteads and on the trail. Includes Wallace Stegner's *The Colt*, about a young horse whose forelegs are broken soon after birth, and how a man tries to rear him for his son, but is eventually forced to abandon the attempt and to have the colt destroyed. Also, Dorothy M. Johnson's *Flame on the Frontier*, the story of two white girls captured and brought up by Indians, and some easy-to-read, less well-known stories, *The Day the Sun Came Out*, *Gold-Mounted Guns* and *The Returning*. A more demanding selection is available in C. E. J. Smith's *Ten Western Stories* (Longman, Imprint Books).

Rowe, Albert *Pollen Girl* Macmillan Education, Rockets

The story of Pollen Girl's adventures when she takes her little brother, Food-in-the-Hand hunting in the forest, including an encounter with a huge, angry bear and a fight with a Crow brave. A book that can be offered to inexperienced readers who have enjoyed the author's *Lone Wolf* (Macmillan Education, Club 75).

Schaefer, Jack *Shane* Heinemann Educational Books, New Windmill

The classic story of the mysterious cowboy hero Shane, told by the boy into whose family corral he rode one summer night in 1889. Other westerns by Jack Schaefer, available in the New Windmill series, are *First Blood* and *The Big Range*, as well as *The Canyon*, the unusual story of the Cheyenne Indian Little Bear, whose conscience makes him always pass the war-pipe unsmoked.

Young, Peter *Dead Man's Trail* Schofield and Sims, Data

For those with a reading age of ten to eleven years. A straight-forward adventure story involving Nick Kane, his sister Jane and his Indian friend Eagle Feather, telling how with Ed Fox, a Texas cowboy, they track down a gang that has held up a stage and rustled a herd of cattle. Also at the same level Peter Young's *Data on Cowboys* (Schofield and Sims).

References

1 DES (1975) *A Language for Life* (Bullock Report) HMSO
2 WHITEHEAD, F. *et al* (1975) 'Children's reading interests' *Schools Council Working Paper 52* Evans/Methuen Educational

6   From remedial to reader

Olive Robinson

Head of the Remedial Department,
Cowley St John Upper School, Oxford

Every secondary school contains a number of pupils who are
called remedial readers because they have not reached a certain
standard in their reading abilities. These children are often
grouped together and given extra, intensive help with reading
for a certain period of time or, in some schools alas, they are all
classified as slow learners and catered for only at a low level and
at a slow pace. These readers, however, are underachieving for
a variety of reasons and if the reasons can be individually
diagnosed and assessed, a more constructive approach can be
made and a development of more adequate skills obtained. The
pupils I shall be writing about in this article form a substantial
part of any group of children referred to a remedial department
in any secondary school. They are those who have been defeated
by circumstance and rendered unmotivated by the time they
have reached secondary level. Unlike slow learners of low ability,
their potential ability is often average, sometimes a little below
and sometimes well above. They are children who might well
have been adequate readers if they had experienced an appropriate and consistent approach to the development of reading
skills from an early age. Often they are those whose abilities
remain underfunctioning because they have a history of illness
causing many and/or long absences from school at a vital age;
or who come from families who have moved a great deal and thus
have been subjected to different methods taught by different
teachers in different schools. Among them too are, notably, a
number who remained at infant school for a period of not more

than five terms – whereas among their age group there are others who were at infant school for six terms or longer and were thus given more valuable time for developing language and cognitive skills, and for forming a consistent and encouraging relationship with an educating adult. It is worthwhile noticing here that this kind of relationship is often missing from the development of children with reading difficulties and also that definite stages in the teaching of skills are often incomplete in their experience or else missing entirely.

Very often these children have to function against a family background that, although concerned, is inadequate educationally; exerting too much pressure in some cases, and in others too ready to accept underachievement until too late. Unstable family backgrounds, too, can contribute to a great extent to a lack of concentration on acquiring reading skills while children have to grapple with the emotional upheaval incurred by divorces, separations, family arguments or even death. The problems faced by the teacher are greatest when an accumulation of these stress factors occurs.

Attitudes

The young child who misses teaching stages for any of the reasons mentioned above, or who is placed in new surroundings with a different teaching approach, is thrown into a state of confusion and tension. Different demands are made on him as he grows, that he hasn't the equipment to cope with. He begins to feel inadequate and unable to function to the required standard and his confidence begins to ebb. If his dilemma is not spotted and dealt with, sympathetically and adequately, at this stage, the nature and extent of his problems increase as he grows older. The gap between his acquisition of skills and the demands made upon him widen and his confidence is further eroded. Emotionally, he feels a failure and his self-esteem is lowered. As he passes through his years in school the reading materials he is given or surrounded by become increasingly difficult and his reaction is one of fear. 'Books are rubbish' he cries, in self-defence. His contemporaries reinforce his sense of failure through their own ability to progress, and behavioural difficulties of many kinds can occur.

Attitudes towards the child are moulded by his behaviour and achievement as he progresses through the school, and the circle is maintained and often reinforced by expectation. So at secondary level this kind of remedial reader arrives with a sense of educated failure, and the teacher often greets him with an educated sense of low expectation. But it is at this stage that steady progress can most easily commence if the remedial teacher resolves to meet each child as an individual, to assess and supply his needs, and shows herself to be concerned about him. The child, on the brink of adolescence at this stage, needs someone to care about him; someone with whom he can relax; someone who accepts his weaknesses and knows where his strengths lie. An encouraging, positive, monitoring relationship can engender confidence and interest. The teacher has to give herself time to learn from the child – each 'failure' of approach must be scrapped and a fresh one made. Each 'success' breeds hope both in child and in teacher. To discover the strong learning areas in each child is the teacher's task and to praise achievement in any form, no matter how irrelevant to reading it appears, is of prime importance. Success and praise give rise to motivation, and success that is given due recognition gives strength to the caring relationship which must occur to sustain that motivation, and which will raise the levels of confidence and self-esteem.

Assessment
Assessment of problems and monitoring of progress are essential ingredients for successful remedial teaching and they are most essential for the children we are considering. A diagnostic reading test is a useful basis from which to start as it presents a reading age upon which the teacher can base her materials. Care should be taken that the reading test will indicate to the teacher something of that which she wishes to know. It should also assess comprehension. Sometimes more than one kind of test should be

used in order to diagnose more clearly the weaknesses and strengths of the child. The teacher will need to define for herself what reading is, and what her aims are, and to devise individualized programmes for the children she teaches, based upon the results of her observations and tests given with due regard to her own aims and the needs of the child. A guide to tests can be found in Stephen Jackson's *A Teacher's Guide to Tests and Testing* (2nd edition) (Longman) and a list of particularly useful tests is given in Appendix B.

All results and diagnoses should be recorded, together with any programme to fill in the gaps thus noted, or, more particularly, to reinforce those areas where the student achieves most and where his motivation is most apparent. Success and failure in any area in the programmes must also be recorded, together with a careful observation of attitudes, moods, interests and reactions. The reading and comprehension tests should be administered at regular intervals, by the same person, and the progress noted. This will show the teacher how well she is succeeding with individual students and will enable her to devise new methods of approach if necessary. Indeed, remedial teaching is more successful if the approaches are varied, even in the direction of reinforcing only one particular skill. This is because a varied approach maintains the pupils' interest and motivation, two prime concerns when lack of concentration has continually to be fought.

These aspects of assessment should be carried out against a background of careful remedial 'counselling' during which the pupil's background, his anxieties, attitudes and problems are openly and honestly discussed. Not only is this therapeutic emotionally for the pupil but it enables him, perhaps for the first time, to begin to use language effectively to communicate the things that affect him most deeply. Many of these pupils have never been encouraged to express their thoughts and feelings and often come from homes where expressive language is inadequate. The use of such language and the opportunity to become meaningfully communicative at this level can be the key to forming the kind of relationship between teacher and pupil upon which remedial teaching must be based. This secure, encouraging relationship must be built up in a relaxed and confident atmosphere and must be given time to develop, free from pressure. At the same time the pupil should be given areas of responsibility in which he can succeed. These may range from something as simple as remembering to bring writing materials to class with him, to giving and receiving telephone messages for the teacher and/or performing responsible jobs around the school.

If the teacher has any kind of anxiety about a medical contributory factor to the child's reading difficulties, then the appropriate medical and/or psychological tests, at whatever level, should be arranged. For instance, sometimes a pupil will succeed only in a small group situation because he is unable to hear properly in a larger class; and a weakness in auditory skill acquisition might well be due to intermittent catarrhal problems.

Organization
There are four ways to organize remedial teaching:

1 Individual – one-to-one teaching.
2 Withdrawing small groups for a certain amount of time per day or per week.
3 Total integration with normal classes with remedial teachers acting in an advisory capacity.
4 Total withdrawal in a remedial class.

Both one, two and three have their place in the total development of reading skills and indeed, in my experience, the use of all three approaches, carefully and individually balanced and monitored, has brought the best results. The fourth approach is not to be advised. It is quite counter-productive as it creates a streamed situation where a class is especially constructed for children who are known or become known as failures. Thus is failure reinforced and motivation discouraged. Very often too a least able teacher is placed with a least able class and can easily become unmotivated herself when faced with a comparatively large number of remedial children. It should be stated firmly that remedial teaching is highly skilled and requires the most diligent, resourceful and imaginative teachers, and remedial pupils themselves deserve the kind of learning situation where their potential abilities can be given the greatest opportunities to develop. Economically and socially society will benefit from such understanding of the underachiever's needs and capabilities.

So the optimum size for a temporarily withdrawn group of remedial pupils would be between five and eight and it is in such groups that the language needs of the pupils can best be catered for. It is while pupils are involved in group work that a teacher can more easily observe, from a non-involved position, the social, language and reading capabilities of individuals and can thus use this valuable time to structure and develop more individualized programmes.

Methods and materials
There is no one particular method of teaching reading. Every pupil can learn better in certain areas than in others and all materials should be geared to meet the individual's needs. Certain apparatus for the teaching and reinforcing of basic phonic and 'whole word' skills is easily obtainable, but the teacher needs always to be able to adapt such materials and vary such games to suit the background and requirements of her pupils. Moreover, she should be prepared to make her own apparatus to consolidate and fit in with the teaching pattern she is using at any given time. This apparatus might be for one individual pupil with specific requirements, or it might be for two or more pupils to use within a group. Such apparatus should be designed to fulfil a relevant purpose and not merely to amuse or to keep students busy. All work in any remedial group should always have a direct and functional purpose that the pupil himself should be aware of as well as the teacher. In being made aware the pupil can be enabled to transfer the purpose of the apparatus to other areas where the same principles are required.

It is necessary to add that, at this secondary level, materials should be not only at an appropriate skill-development level, but also at an appropriate emotional level, and should in addition be self-correcting wherever possible. An important aim is to make the pupil responsible for his own progress and independent in his use of materials. All progress should be noted and recorded. Use of 'cloze' procedure material helps the teacher to assess comprehension and reading and also aids the development of speculative ability, frequently an area of weakness in pupils who experience reading difficulties.

There are, therefore, almost as many ways of teaching reading as there are pupils, but a common sharing of language, excitement in its use and a sense of language purpose and achievement are of paramount importance. Group work is especially good for this kind of activity. The teacher must be able to perceive what activates the pupils' interests and start from there, concentrating on bringing all of the senses into use and translating the awakening awareness of the pupils into language, both oral and written; reinforcing their concentrated experience with relevant extracts from books. This sharing of experience, not only with each other but with another – writer, explorer, or whatever character from the world of books – can be a revelation to the developing adolescent and will often reawaken the curiosity and desire for finding out things that have been lost, or more accurately, submerged, in the period when he became an 'educated failure'. If the feeling he has against books is very strong the pupil can create his own, using his own words (no matter how ungrammatical initially), providing his own illustrations and diagrams, which he can draw or cut out from magazines, and decorating his own book jacket. This way into reading has been successfully used with some most reluctant pupils.

The teacher again therefore has to know all of her pupils well, and in addition she has to be well organized and know all her materials. She must be particularly alive to the developing needs of the pupils and not make the mistake of keeping them within one area of any activity for too long. Stimulus material on film, on slides and on tape can always be used to great advantage with those pupils whose motivation in the use of language is weak and who are not able to concentrate for too long on the written or printed word. Use of these audio-visual aids should be independent and a small group of pupils can impress teachers by their ability to record, and edit, original plays, spontaneous stories, discussions and a variety of highly inventive word and sound games. Cameras too can be used effectively, with photographs taken by the group shown in a scrap book with taped information about each picture attached to the book for other groups to play. The tape is then transcribed and a new group book produced. This kind of activity inspires other groups and individuals to new ventures, which often eventually lead to the use of 'real' books for ideas for true-life stories and for further knowledge on the use of equipment and so on.

Books should be as widely based as possible giving a broad range of subjects, both fiction and non-fiction. There is now a greater choice on the market of books suitable for slower readers, but books should always be chosen with great care. They should be well illustrated and the layout should be clear and attractive with as much attention paid to the space around the print as is given to the typeface itself. The material in the books should be relevant and well presented. It should not be written in a patronizing manner and should sound natural and appropriate to an adolescent level when read aloud. A short list of books at the end of this article gives some examples that have proved both popular and effective.

It is obviously important that the teacher should know the books that she supplies and that she should base her decision to buy them on several criteria. I have already mentioned the layout of books, but the teacher must also be familiar with the content and language levels of them, and learn to match these against her pupils' needs. The readability of books is often discussed now and it is worthwhile spending time and effort in assessing this in order to commit money wisely and with as little wastage as possible. It can be done with the aid of published guides on readability. One such guide is *The Fog Index*,[1] and another is *Fry's Readability Graph*.[2] The results obtained using these guides, however, must be treated cautiously as the process used is necessarily mechanical, and the language of the pupil, and his social and cultural environment, must always be given due consideration. The final decision on whether or not to buy rests on the likes and dislikes of the pupil and the teacher's awareness of stimulus and need.

In the group, it is desirable that each student should select his own reading book. Of course the teacher should always encourage him to move on to others that will cater for expanding interests and skills; but at the same time she should not encourage him to choose books that are too difficult. Rather she should direct him to books that will cater for the same interests but at an appropriate reading level.

Reading levels are generally regarded as falling into three categories:

1 Independent level – at which the student can read material with ninety-nine per cent accuracy.
2 Instructional level – material is read by the student with ninety-five per cent accuracy.
3 Frustration level – material is read by the student with less than ninety per cent accuracy.

It is at the third stage that a pupil can again become so discouraged, with a reading level of ten or more words in each hundred read wrongly, and a comprehension level considerably lower, that he can fall back again into that unmotivated, reluctant state that brought him to the remedial teacher in the first instance.

Teachers can in the secondary school, however, help the remedial pupil to use necessary reference books more easily by guiding him on tape through appropriate pages and paragraphs, and by using a synchrofax machine for reading aloud pages containing the required information.

At all times the teacher should be understanding, patient and firm, helping the pupil to discover his own needs and reasons for reading; and she should be prepared continually to evaluate her own methods and progress with individual pupils.

The remedial teacher cannot work in isolation if she is to help the pupils in her care to achieve. An adolescent should not be totally withdrawn from other areas of activity around the school, but the teacher should none the less be aware of the continuation of his remedial needs. To this end she must be prepared to work in close co-operation with other members of staff. In this way she can advise on presentation of materials in other subjects and, if necessary, adapt them to the required level. She can also advise on pupils' attitudes and learning problems and enable staff to gain understanding and insight into their needs. Observing remedial children in classrooms coping, or not coping, with different situations and problems, can also be of great value to the remedial teacher; she will learn from the pupil new aspects of his problems and, if she is wise, will take them into consideration when meeting him in a small group or in a 'counselling' session.

A pupil with reading difficulties is thus catered for in all aspects of his school life, and if he is given the opportunity to express himself and is accepted as a person with problems rather than as a failure, he can begin to discover an ability within himself to cope. It can become possible for him to begin to articulate his ambitions and define his aims, and the more he is encouraged in the independent use of language, the more possible it becomes for him to think about the nature of his problems and fit them into the context of the world about him. It is essential at this stage for the teacher to give him as much support and encouragement as possible. As he becomes more motivated to succeed, so he deserves praise and encouragement, no matter at what basic level he achieves success.

Reading material for a pupil who is beginning to succeed must still be selected with care and he must not be expected to proceed too quickly. He will still need interest and encouragement, and to be given a broad selection of books to choose from, if he is not to lapse in his newly-acquired skills. A student who is making good progress with remedial help is in a vulnerable situation. He can so easily lose confidence and self-esteem again if teachers expect too much of him and push him too far, at a pace that his newly discovered capabilities cannot keep up with. Similarly, his confidence and feeling of security need to be maintained within a firm framework of learning. In this way his progress is monitored and he will slowly respond. Each small success should be built upon, so that the student delights in achievement and is not downcast in the disappointment of failure.

Notes

1 Obtainable from the Centre for the Teaching of Reading, University of Reading School of Education, 29 Eastern Avenue, Reading, Berkshire
2 An adaptation of this graph is to be found in the BBC *Adult Literary Handbook* (1975) BBC Publications

Appendix A
Three case studies

Throughout: reading test – *Neale Analysis of Reading Ability;* verbal and non-verbal reasoning tests – NFER.

1 Katy

Referred September 1975; age eleven years three months; reading age eight years seven months; comprehension eight years seven months.

Katy was a quiet and withdrawn girl who had a squint and a mild speech impediment. She was very shy and responded only in a one-to-one situation. Over a period of three months she progressed to a reading age of eight years eleven months. During this time it was decided to refer her to an audiologist, a speech therapist and to the educational psychologist. An interview with her parents showed them to be very concerned and they reported a difficult birth. Medical reports showed her hearing was unimpaired but speech therapy was suggested. Sight in her left eye was defective. The psychologist referred her to a paediatrician and brain damage was diagnosed. This was later confirmed by various records sent from the part of the country where Katy was born and had spent her first few years. She had a verbal reasoning quotient of seventy-five and the prognosis was poor. It was decided to concentrate on a one-to-one approach to boost confidence and to encourage self-awareness and self-esteem. The teacher was convinced there was an untapped potential. Interests were discovered, responsibility given and the parents were interviewed regularly. Appropriate book lists were sent home and a follow-up programme was devised for school. Other members of staff were informed and a positive, encouraging attitude was adopted by all who met her.

By July 1976: age twelve years one month; reading age eleven years six months; comprehension eleven years.

Katy is now a lively, articulate girl whose parents are delighted with her progress. She now attends remedial reading groups twice a week and the rest of the time she spends in a normal class where her work is monitored by the remedial teacher. The work is normal class work given under the supervision of the class teacher but advice on the presentation of material comes from the remedial teacher.

Katy's case is unique and is included for that reason. More typical are the two following cases.

2 Colin

Referred April 1975; age twelve years ten months; reading age eight years nine months; comprehension eight years eight months; verbal reasoning ninety-five; non-verbal reasoning ninety-seven.

Colin was referred because his reading age did not match his verbal reasoning level. He was reported variously as being 'lazy', 'disruptive' and 'non-cooperative'.

His father had left home when Colin was four years old and he had spent five terms only in an infant school in another part of the country. Since then he had been to three other schools. He lived with his mother and sister and spent a great deal of time cycling. Often his mother did not know where he was. He resented authority and found it difficult to form relationships, particularly with adults. His mother expressed concern but felt inadequate in coping with him. She could not enforce discipline. He was found to be lacking in auditory skill development, being unable to blend consonants and unable to analyze and synthesize words. A programme of work was devised for him which included a lot of taped sounds, words and music, with gaps on the tapes for him to record guesses at what the noises were, and to record his reactions to the words, stories and music. Apparatus included self-correcting word jigsaws, phonic and word puzzles and games (individual and group), and 'cloze' material. In talks with the teacher it was discovered that his real interests lay not in cycling, but in playing in a wood near his home and, in particular, on and around an oak tree that he called 'Big Dad'. He was interested in the wild life around the tree. When talking of this his language was good and vivid. The tapes he was using were changed to include descriptions and sounds of wild life and relevant books were found for him. He also wrote and illustrated his own book on 'Big Dad'.

By April 1976: age thirteen years ten months; reading age eleven years nine months; comprehension eleven years three months.

Colin is now coping adequately in normal lessons and is doing particularly well at English. His behaviour is now 'normal'. His mother is pleased.

144

3 Jocelyn

Referred September 1976; age thirteen years one month; reading age nine years; comprehension nine years three months; verbal reasoning eighty; non-verbal reasoning ninety-six.

Jocelyn was referred because of the discrepancy between her verbal and non-verbal reasoning levels and because of her low reading age. It was felt that she had language problems.

Jocelyn is West Indian, born in Trinidad; her parents speak with a West Indian structure and intonation, and Jocelyn grew up against this language background. Her reading appeared adequate but she was disinterested and without motivation. He parents were anxious that Jocelyn should do well and were buying her books that were far too difficult, and of inappropriate subject content. It was decided to concentrate on a total approach with as much oral language as possible. The parents were advised to stop buying books and to allow Jocelyn to join a library. She was given a list of books and the parents' help was enlisted to make sure that Jocelyn read for half an hour each evening.

At school, a set of slides and pictures were collected for Jocelyn and she taped what she saw in them, felt about them and so on. The tapes were discussed by Jocelyn and the teacher and story constructions were made from them. 'Cloze' material was given and Jocelyn became very successful with her handwriting and sentence construction and subsequently became very motivated towards writing. She then became interested in writing plays which she and a group of friends would perform on tape. These were sometimes (at her instigation) played to a group and criticised.

By April 1977: age thirteen years eight months; reading age twelve years four months; comprehension twelve years nine months.

Jocelyn now wants to take a CSE examination and is making steady progress.

Appendix B
Useful diagnostic tests

(1958) *Neale Analysis of Reading Ability:* Macmillan

Individual test; six to twelve years; test for speed, accuracy and comprehension.

CARVER, C. (1964) *Word Recognition Test;* University of London Press

Individual or group test; five to eight and a half years; errors made give diagnostic information.

(1970) *GAP Reading Comprehension Test:* Heinemann

Group test; 7·6 to 12·6 years; 'cloze' procedure – child reads silently and fills in missing word.

GAPADOL Reading Comprehension Test: Heinemann

As previous test but for age group twelve to seventeen.

Reading Test EH 1–3: National Foundation for Educational Research

Group test; tests vocabulary, comprehension and speed; eleven to fifteen years.

For a more detailed diagnosis of auditory and visual perceptual difficulties the information given in A. E. Tansley's *Reading and Remedial Reading* (Routledge and Kegan Paul) is of value, as is Kirk, McCarthy and Kirk's *Illinois Test of Psycholinguistic Abilities* (Second Edition) (National Foundation for Educational Research).

Appendix C
Book list

A small selection of the kind of series that have proved to be useful in stimulating and sustaining interest in secondary remedial readers.

Adventures in Space; McCullagh, S.; Hart-Davis

Twelve attractively presented books for nine-year-olds and upwards with reading age of eight to ten.

Banjo, Club and Disco Books; Various authors; Cassell

Three sets of books which appeal to certain children aged twelve and upwards with reading age of six plus to nine.

Booster Books; Chalk, W. C. H.; Heinemann Educational Books

Very popular story books, phonically biased, for eleven-year-olds and upwards with reading age of eight plus to eleven and a half.

Club 75; Various authors; Chambers, A. (ed); Macmillan Education

Eighteen books of stories of interest for boys and girls aged twelve and upwards with reading age of ten to twelve.

Crown Street Kings; Oates, Anne; Macmillan Education

Eighteen lively story books for ten-year-olds and upwards with reading age of nine plus.

Headlines; Various authors; Foster, J. L. (ed); Edward Arnold

Four non-fiction titles about daredevils, remarkable animals, record-breakers and survivors at sea. For nine-year-olds and upwards with reading age of nine plus.

Help Books; Webster, J.; Nelson

First Helpings – six books
Help Story Books – six books
Help Yourself Books – six books
Help Books – six books
Series of books with consistent and extending vocabulary, plus
workbooks, for those with reading age of seven plus.

Inner Ring; Various authors; Benn

First, Second and Third Series – story books for nine- to thirteen-
year-olds.
Sports Series – eight books
True Stories – four books
Facts and Science Series – five books
Pocket Books – four books
Hipsters – for eleven- to thirteen-plus-year-olds with reading age of
eight plus.

Inside and Outside Books; Various authors; Oxford University Press

Eight clearly presented information books on general topics for nine-
year-olds and upwards with reading age of eight and a half to nine
and a half.

Inswinger and Popswinger; Gregory G. and Ward, R.; Hulton

Inswinger (a continuing football story) – six books
Popswinger – four books
For twelve-year-olds and upwards with reading age of eight and a
half plus.

Joan Tate Books; Tate, Joan; Heinemann Educational Books

Eighteen books for eleven-year-olds and upwards with reading age of
nine to twelve.

Ladder Books; Various authors; Oxford University Press

Set of five reference books for remedial and reluctant readers aged
nine and upwards with reading age of nine to ten.

Lively Readers; Sealey, L.; Nelson

Sixteen well-illustrated, graded information books for nine-year-olds and upwards with reading age of eight and upwards.

Onward Paperbacks; Crosher, C. R.; Cassell

Four titles with immediate attraction for boys aged eleven and upwards with reading age of eight and a half to nine and a half.

Solos; Wood, Kathleen; Hart-Davis

Eight highly recommended story books for twelve-year-olds and upwards with reading age of seven to nine.

Trend Books; Various authors; Ginn

Approach Trend – six books for those with reading age of six and a half to seven and a half.
Mainstream Trend – thirty-two books for those with reading age of eight to twelve years.
Trend Set – four books for those with reading age of eight to twelve.
Very popular series of story books covering a wide variety of topics. Suitable for eleven- to sixteen-year-olds.

Sources of information

John L. Foster

Keeping up-to-date with books which might appeal to children of secondary school age is a difficult and time-consuming task even for the dedicated teacher and librarian. In this section details are given of a number of review sources, critical journals, organizations and book clubs that can prove helpful. There is also a list of publishers' addresses and a bibliography giving details of other books on reading which students, teachers and librarians might find useful.

Review sources

Reviewsheet (monthly)

A cheap, duplicated booklet dealing with new fiction, hardback and paperback, suitable for nine- to sixteen-year-olds, started by two Sheffield teachers, Jane Powell and Steve Bowles. The reviewers take as their criterion the question, 'Will this book be enjoyed?' being interested not so much in 'Great Literature' as 'what the kids will like, accepting Daniel Fader's credo that they should read anything, anything to get them "hooked on books" '. Subscription details from Jane Powell, Sydenham School, Dartmouth Road, London se 26.

School Bookshop News (three times a year)

A magazine originally published by Penguin Books, providing information about books and writers and about television and film tie-ins. An invaluable aid for anyone running a school bookshop. Available from the School Bookshop Association, National Book League, 7 Albermarle Street, London WIX 4BB.

School Librarian (quarterly)

Includes articles on librarianship, books and authors as well as reviews. Subscription details from the School Library Association, Victoria House, 29-31 George Street, Oxford OX1 2AY.

Teaching English (three times a year)

A magazine of articles on language and English teaching published by the Centre for Information on the Teaching of English at Moray House College of Education. The review section covers books for the slow learner and reluctant reader as well as recent English textbooks. Subscription details from CITE, Moray House College of Education, Holyrood Road, Edinburgh EH8 8AQ.

Times Educational Supplement (weekly)

Regularly reviews children's fiction and includes occasional articles on reluctant readers. There is a Children's Book Supplement three times a year.

Times Literary Supplement – Children's Books Supplement (quarterly)

Articles and reviews on fiction and non-fiction for children of all ages. It is possible to take out a separate annual subscription to the TLS for the four children's book issues only. Details from the Subscription Department, Times Newspapers Ltd., New Printing House Square, Gray's Inn Road, London WC1X 8EZ.

Critical journals

Children's literature in education (quarterly)

A journal devoted to the discussion of children's books. Since its first appearance in 1970 it has provided a forum for writers to explore the challenges and choices involved in writing for children, for critics to discuss approaches to the study and evaluation of children's literature, and for teachers to describe and to analyze their classroom practices. A selection of some of the more significant articles that have appeared in *Children's Literature in Education* has been published in the book, *Writers, Critics and Children* (Heinemann Educational Books, 1976) edited by Geoff Fox. Subscription details from CLE, 3 Elsynge Road, London SW18.

Signal (three times a year)

Published by Aidan and Nancy Chambers this magazine consists of articles on a wide variety of topics concerned with children and books. There are, for example, reprints of nineteenth-and early-twentieth century writings on books for children, edited by Lance Salway, and articles on illustrators and children's bookshops, as well as on contemporary authors, the criticism of children's literature and current trends. Subscription details from the editor, Nancy Chambers, The Thimble Press, Lockwood, Station Road, South Woodchester, Glos GL5 5EQ.

Organizations

Centre for the Teaching of Reading

A unit of the University of Reading School of Education which houses a permanent collection of reading materials, including books for the reluctant teenage reader. There is a separate display of books for the adult non-reader, many of which can also be used with the older secondary pupil. The centre acts as a 'clearing house' for ideas and information on all aspects of the teaching of reading and publishes a number of inexpensive booklets such as *Retarded and Reluctant Readers: Graded Lists of Selected Books for Secondary School Pupils* compiled by Bridie Raban and Wendy Body. A full list of publications and prices is obtainable from Betty Root, Tutor-in-Charge, Centre for the Teaching of Reading, University of Reading School of Education, 29 Eastern Avenue, Reading, Berks RG1 5RU.

National Association for the Teaching of English

Concerns itself with all aspects of English teaching and language development. Members receive three copies per year of the journal, *English in Education*, containing articles on language theory and classroom practice that are often of interest to teachers of reluctant readers. The annual conference, held at Easter, usually has a commission exploring some aspect of reading at the secondary level. In 1976 the author Geraldine Kaye led a workshop group on 'Writing for Children' and in 1977 Jane Powell and Louise Barry organized a study group on 'Children's Literature'. Membership details from National Association for the Teaching of English, 10B Thornhill Road, Edgerton, Huddersfield HD3 3AU.

National Association of Remedial Education

Organizes courses and discussion groups on the problems of pupils in need of help with their reading. It has also published several useful books, such as *The A–Z of Reading*, which includes a section giving an assessment of the readability level of books for the slower secondary reader based on the Spache Readability Test, and *A Classroom Index of Phonic Resources*. Details of publications and of membership from the National Association of Remedial Education, 4 Old Croft Road, Walton-on-the-Hill, Stafford.

National Book League

Organizes a number of travelling exhibitions of books for the slow, backward and reluctant reader. Two of the annotated guides, *Starting Point: Books for the Illiterate Adult and Older Reluctant Reader* by Betty Root and Sue Brownhill and *Help in*

Reading by Stanley S. Segal and Tom Pascoe, are useful surveys indicating interest levels and reading ages of books in many of the available series. Full list of publications and membership details from the National Book League, 7 Albermarle Street, London W1X 4BB.

School Bookshop Association

Formed in 1976 to co-ordinate and develop the school bookshop movement and to cater for the 4,000 school bookshops already in existence. Produces a termly magazine, *School Bookshop News*, and offers advice on running a bookshop, including information on suppliers, layout, stocktaking and staffing. Membership details from the School Bookshop Association, National Book League, 7 Albermarle Street, London W1X 4BB.

School Library Association

Concerned with all aspects of the organization of books and resources in schools. There are many flourishing local branches which run short courses, arrange talks by authors and circulate review sheets compiled by members. There is a biennial national conference and members receive the *School Librarian* quarterly. Details from the School Library Association, Victoria House, 29–31 George Street, Oxford OX1 2AY.

United Kingdom Reading Association

An association for all those interested in the teaching of reading skills at any level. Members receive the journal *Reading* three times a year and there is an annual study conference every summer. Membership and subscription details from S. V. Heatlie, Hon. General Secretary UKRA, 63 Laurel Grove, Sunderland, County Durham, SR2 9EE.

To join all the national organizations listed above on an individual basis would be a costly business, but they offer institutional membership whereby schools and colleges can join. Although less money is available than formerly, if reading is a matter of real concern, then membership of such organizations should remain a priority. Their publications are a useful means of disseminating ideas throughout a department and the courses they run make a valuable contribution to the in-service training of teachers. The advantage of being an individual member is that you receive your own copy of the publications.

Book clubs

Obviously the best way of selling books to children is to run a school bookshop. Often, however, this proves administratively difficult, although the problems can frequently be overcome more easily than many teachers realize, and before rejecting the idea of running a bookshop it is worth contacting the School Bookshop Association (see page 154) for advice. Alternative methods of giving children an opportunity to buy books are organizing book fairs and running book clubs. Book fairs can be made into special occasions by involving parents, by inviting an expert to describe the books available or an author to talk about his writing and to read from his books, or by organizing special events. One highly successful book fair recently had, amongst other attractions, a book maze.

Book clubs are easier for the hard-pressed teacher to run than book fairs. The chief drawback is that the choice of books is much more limited. But they are a means of bringing books within the reach of those children who rarely, if ever, visit a bookshop.

The Bookworm Club

A paperback club for eight- to twelve-year-olds. Pupils receive a four-page *Bookworm Bulletin* twice a term. There are club extras for the children and a ten per cent cash bonus for the school on the value of all books ordered. Details from The

Bookworm Club, Napier Place, Cumbernauld, Glasgow G69 ODN.

Puffin School Book Club

The books available are described in attractive full-colour leaflets, *Puffin Book Club News*, mailed to schools six times a year. Each issue contains a selection of pupils' letters and contributions from authors are also published. Orders are sent to one of the regional booksellers participating in the scheme. Full details from the Development Unit, Penguin Books Ltd., Harmondsworth, Middlesex UB7 ODA.

Scene Club

A club for pupils of twelve and over, offering a selection of more adult books than those offered by either the Bookworm or Puffin Clubs. There is a pupil dividend scheme and a free book for the club organizer with every order. Details and samples of *Scene Club News* from Scholastic Publications, Westfield Road, Southam, Leamington Spa, Warwickshire CV33 OJH.

Bibliography
The books I have included are those that I have found particularly useful in formulating my ideas about reading and reluctance to read.

CALTHROP, K. (1971) *Reading Together* Heinemann Educational Books
CHAMBERS, A. (1969) *The Reluctant Reader* Pergamon Press
CHAMBERS, A. (1973) *Introducing Books to Children* Heinemann Educational Books
D'ARCY, P. (1973) *Reading for Meaning* (especially Volume II 'The reader's response') Hutchinson
FADER, D. (1969) *Hooked on Books* Pergamon Press
FOX, G. *et al* (1976) *Writers, Critics and Children* Heinemann Educational Books

HILDICK, E. W. (1970) *Children and Fiction* Evans
HOLLINDALE, P. (1974) *Choosing Books for Children* Paul Elek
KOHL, H. (1974) *Reading, How To* Penguin
LAWRENCE, D. (1973) *Improved Reading Through Counselling* Ward Lock Educational
LONGLEY, C. (ed) *Reading After Ten* BBC Publications
MEEK, M. *et al* (eds) (1976) *The Cool Web* Bodley Head
MOON, C. and RABAN, B. (1975) *A Question of Reading* Ward Lock Educational
REID, J. F. (ed) (1972) *Reading: Problems and Practices* Ward Lock Educational
TOWNSEND, J. R. (1971) *A Sense of Story* Longman
WALKER, C. (1974) *Reading Development and Extension* Ward Lock Educational
WHITEHEAD, F. *et al* (1975) 'Children's reading interests' *Schools Council Working Paper 52* Evans/Methuen Educational

List of Publishers addresses

Abelard-Schuman Ltd., 450 Edgware Road, London W2 1EG
Arnold, Edward (Publishers) Ltd., Woodlands Park Avenue, Maidenhead, Berks.
BBC Publications, 35 Marylebone High Street, London W1M 4AA
Benn, Ernest Ltd., Sovereign Way, Tonbridge, Kent
Blackie and Sons Ltd., Bishopbriggs, Glasgow G64 2NZ
Bodley Head Ltd., 9 Bow Street, Covent Garden, London WC2 7AL
Brockhampton Press Ltd., Salisbury Road, Leicester (Now Hodder and Stoughton Children's Books.)
Cassell & Collier-Macmillan Ltd., 35 Red Lion Square, London WC1R 4SG
Chatto & Windus Ltd., 40–42 William IV Street, London WC2E 9BR.
Chivers, Cedric Ltd., Portway, Bath BA1 3NF
Collins, William Sons & Co. Ltd., 144 Cathedral Street, Glasgow G4 ONB
Dent, J. M. & Sons Ltd., 10 Bedford Street, London WC2E 9RB
Deutsch, André Ltd., 105 Great Russell Street, London WC1B 3LJ
Dobson Book Ltd., 80 Kensington Church Street, London W8
Elek, Paul, 54–58 Caledonian Road, London N1 9RN
Evans Brothers Ltd., Montague House, Russell Square, London WC1
Faber & Faber Ltd., 3 Queen Square, London WC1

Futura Publications Ltd., 49 Poland Street, London WIA 2LG

Ginn & Co. Ltd., Elsinore House, Buckingham Street, Aylesbury, Bucks.

Gollancz (Victor) Ltd., 14 Henrietta Street, London WC2E 8QJ

Hamish Hamilton Ltd., 90 Great Russell Street, London WCI 3PT

Hamlyn Group, 42 The Centre, Feltham, Middlesex

Hart-Davis Educational Ltd., Frogmore, St Albans, Herts.

Heinemann Educational Books Ltd., 48 Charles Street, Mayfair, London WIX 8AH

Heinemann Young Books, 15 Queen Street, Mayfair, London WIX 8BE

Hodder & Stoughton, St Paul's House, Warwick Lane, London EC4

Hulton Educational Publications Ltd., Raans Road, Amersham, Bucks.

Hutchinson Educational, Tiptree, Colchester, Essex

Longman Group Ltd., Longman House, Burnt Mill, Harlow, Essex

Lutterworth Press, Luke House, Farnham Road, Guildford, Surrey

Macdonald & Evans Ltd., Estover Road, Plymouth PL6 7PZ

Macmillan Education Ltd, 4 Little Essex Street, London WC2 3LF

Nelson, Thomas & Sons Ltd., Lincoln Way, Windmill Road, Sunbury-on-Thames, Middlesex TW16 7HP

Oliver & Boyd, Croythorn House, 23 Ravelstone Terrace, Edinburgh EH4 3TJ

Oxford University Press, Walton Street, Oxford

Pan Books Ltd., Cavaye Place, London SW10 9PG

Penguin Books Ltd., Harmondsworth, Middlesex UB7 ODA

Pergamon Press Ltd., see A. Wheaton and Co.

Schofield and Sims Ltd., 35 St John's Road, Huddersfield HDI 5DT

Scholastic Publications Ltd., Westfield Road, Southam, Leamington Spa, Warwickshire CV33 OJH

Tandem, see Wyndham Publications Ltd.

Transworld Publishers Ltd., Cavendish House, 57–59 Uxbridge
    Road, London w5.
Ward Lock Educational, 116 Baker Street, London wIM 2BB
Wheaton, A. & Co., Hennock Road, Exeter EX2 8RP
Wyndham Publications Ltd., 123 King Street, London w6 9JG

Index

accent, discrimination by 41–2
Across the Barricades (Lingard) 118
Adams, Philippa 84
Admission to The Feast (Beckman) 85
adolescent stories 74–7
adventure stories 77–84
Adventures in Space series (Hart-Davis) 147
Aerial series (Chivers) 121
After the Raft Race (MacGibbon) 119
Aiken, Joan 123
Air Hostess Ann (Hawken) 47
Alcott, Louisa M. 46
Alderson, Jim 97
All in the Game (Gillett) 116
All Quiet on the Western Front (Remarque) 127
Allen, Mabel Ester 78
Allen, Richard 4
Alvarez, Al 2
American novels 46–7, 56, 60–1, 62
Andra (Lawrence) 109
Andrew, Prudence 61, 78, 117
Answering Miss Roberts (Leach) 76
anthologies 3
Arkley, Arthur J. 98, 108
Armstrong, Richard 47
Arnold, Matthew 7
Arundel, Honor 46, 58, 60, 84, 87, 88, 99, 118
Asimov, Isaac 104, 105
Ask For King Billy (Treece) 124
assessment *see* testing
Athena series (Wheaton) 73
Athletics Champions (Foster) 115
Away From Home (Hardcastle) 113

Backwater War (Woodford) 125
Bad Lot, A (Glanville) 112
Bagley, Desmond 121
Baker, Geoffrey 74, 84
Ballard, J. G. 104
Ballard, Martin 61, 113, 117
Banjo series (Cassell) 148

Banks, Lynne Reid 51, 52, 56, 99, 102, 103
Barry, Margaret Stuart 78
Barstow, Stan 19, 74, 88, 93
Basketball Game, The (Lester) 51, 62
Bateman, Robert 110
Bates, H. E. 126
Baudouy, Michel-Aimé 111
Bawden, Nina 53, 127
Bebbington, Roy 121
Beckman, Gunnel 57, 59, 71, 85
Before Eden (Clarke) 108
Behan, Brendan 93
Belstone Fox, The (Rook) 24
Benedict, Rex 129
Berman, Lucy 97
Bess (Leeson) 63
Bevis (Jefferies) 20–1
Big One, The (Hardcastle) 71
Big Range, The (Schaeffer) 130
Bike Racers, The (Carter) 110–11
Billy Liar (Waterhouse and Hall) 88
biography 69, 70
Bionic Man and *Bionic Woman* books 104
Birdy and the Group (Hildick) 80
Birdy in Amsterdam (Hildick) 80
Birdy Jones (Hildick) 80
Birdy Swings North (Hildick) 80
Blackboard Jungle, The (Hunter) 6, 91
Blair Immel, Mary 75
Blake, Quentin 11
Blast Off At Woomera (Walters) 109
Bless the Beasts and Children (Swarthout) 90
Blinder, The (Hines) 112
Blish, James 106
Blood Feud (Sutcliff) 62
Blyton, Enid 20, 78
Boat and Bax, A (Collinson) 79
Bond, James 23, 121
book clubs 155–6
booklist, by subject 72–131

161

Rockets series (Macmillan) 53, 77
Rodman, Maria 89
Rogue Male (Household) 123
Rook, David 24
Rose Red (Heywood) 87
Rosenberg, Sandra 77
Rough Shoot, A (Household) 123
Rowe, Albert 129, 130
Rowe Townsend, John 55, 61, 83, 103
Rumblefish (Hinton) 92
Run For Your Life (Line) 123–4
Run to the Mountain (Paice) 93, 95
Runaways, The (Canning) 123
Running Blind (Bagley) 121
Running Hot and Cold (Baker) 84–5
Running Scared (Evans) 122
Rutherford, Douglas 114
Ruum, The (Porges) 108
Rx for Tomorrow (Nourse) 108

Salinger, J. D. 6, 90
Sam and Me (Tate) 55, 73, 103
Sampson, Fay 21
Sargeson, Frank 98
Saunders, Jean 85, 87, 120, 124
Savage God, The (Alvarez) 2
Save the Last Dance for Me (Carew) 96, 105
Saville, Malcolm 78
Scene (*formerly* Scoop Club) 156
Schaeffer, Jack 130
School Bookshop Association 154
School Bookshop News 150–1
school bookshops 10, 31, 150–1, 155
School Librarian 151
School Library Association 154
Schools Council 67, 68–9
science fiction stories 104–9
Scillies Trip, The (Branfield) 60
Scoop Club (*now* Scene) 156
Scorpio Letters, The (Canning) 121
Scott, Rachel 87
Sea Change (Armstrong) 47
Sealey, L. 147
Search for Susan (Boyers) 76
Searching for Skylights (Leach) 76, 118
Season in Europe (Wilson) 115
Second Chance for Love (Leete) 71
selective reading 3–4
Sell-Out (Maddock) 59, 74, 76–7
Selvon, Samuel 112
September Song (Martin) 101–2
Serraillier, Ian 127
Seventeen Oranges (Naughton) 81, 82
Seventeen Seconds (Southall) 126
Seventeenth Summer (Daly) 47, 100
Sewell, Anna 20
sexual topics 55–8

Shakespeare, William 2, 6–7
Shane (Schaeffer) 130
Sherburne, Zoa 98
Sherry, Sylvia 94, 100, 128
Shoot (football magazine) 110
short stories 26, 78–9, 80–1, 82, 83, 86–7, 90, 91, 92, 93
    ghost 95–9
    love 100–1
    science fiction 105, 108, 109
    sport 111–12
    war 126–7
    western 129, 130
Siege at Robin's Hill (Dickenson) 6, 87, 94
Signal 152
Sillitoe, Alan 88, 93
Sillitoe Selection, A 93
Silver Sword, The (Serraillier) 127
Since That Party (Brattstrom) 86
Sinstadt, Gerald 111
Six, The (Green) 52, 91
Six Summers (Robinson) 102
Sixteen (Daly) 100
Skinhead (Allen) 4, 11, 89
Sky High (Baker) 74
Slug, The (Hoyland) 91
small print 11
Smith, C. E. J. 129, 130
Smith, V. 79
Smuggler, The (Plowright) 124
Snake River (Chambers) 129
Snatched (Parker) 122
Snow Goose, The (Gallico) 128
social-realist writing 43–4
Social Work for Jill (Cochrane) 47
Solos series (Hart-Davis) 53, 148
Sons and Lovers (Lawrence) 20
Soul Brothers and Sister Lou, The (Hunter) 62
Southall, Ivan 126
Space Hostages (Fisk) 108
Space 1999 books 104
Spaceship Medic (Harrison) 108
Speed Six (Carter) 114
Sperry, Armstrong 83
Spider Bomb, The (Chalk) 126
Spillane, Mickey 72
Spirals series (Hutchinson) 53
Spirals (Jackson) 97, 105
sports stories 109–15
    sport non-fiction 115–6
Sports Stories (Foster ed.) 111–12
Spray of Leaves (Chilton) 107
Stage to Nowhere (Hirst) 129
Stamboul Train (Greene) 51
Star Trek books 104
Starting Point, The (Kamm) 118